AF530320

# 4 PILLARS

# OF

# INNER PEACE

**A Journey to Inner Harmony and Emotional Freedom**

**DR.MUNEER JAN**

**For my mother,**

**Rajbi**

# Table of Contents

# PREFACE

## Four Pillars of Inner Peace

The ICU is a unique place where life and death meet daily, filled with stories of struggle and resilience. Working there has shaped my clinical skills and understanding of life. It's a space of both hope and sadness, where compassion and deep connections highlight the fragility of existence.

Over the years, I carried the emotional weight of caring for critically ill patients and supporting their families. This often led to stress, but I eventually learned that finding inner peace was essential to navigating these challenges.

Inner peace doesn't mean being free from difficulties. Instead, it’s about finding clarity, empathy, and resilience during tough times. My journey has led me to discover four key principles: Saying Sorry, Forgiveness, Gratitude, and Love. These principles have changed my life and helped me maintain balance in a chaotic world.

1. **Saying Sorry**: Acknowledging our mistakes and apologizing can strengthen relationships and promote healing. I've learned that admitting faults is a sign of strength.

2. **Forgiveness**: Letting go of anger and resentment is crucial. I've witnessed families finding peace in moments of forgiveness, which showed me that it’s as much a gift to ourselves as it is to others.

3. **Gratitude**: Appreciating the small blessings in life brings joy. In the ICU, I've seen patients find happiness in simple moments, reminding me to practice gratitude daily.

4. **Love**: Love is the ultimate source of meaning and connection. It motivates us to care for one another and helps us endure tough times. In my work, I've witnessed love overcoming fear and pain.

These four pillars—Saying Sorry, Forgiveness, Gratitude, and Love—serve as practical guides for leading a more harmonious and fulfilling life. This book, Four Pillars of Inner Peace, explores these principles and reflects my professional journey while inviting others to seek harmony, whether facing challenges or desiring a deeper sense of purpose. Life is unpredictable, but we can build a foundation for peace amid its uncertainties.

# Introduction

## The Pursuit of Inner Peace in Modern Life

Inner Peace is a universal desire, yet it often feels just out of reach.

In this high-speed connectivity, social media, and endless materialistic pursuits, people usually correlate inner peace with external achievements— a high-paying job, luxury, or social validation. However, true inner peace is much deeper than material success. Studies in positive psychology reveal long-term Inner Peace is rooted in emotional well-being, meaningful connections, and a sense of purpose.

Despite advancements in technology and comfort, depression and anxiety have reached epidemic proportions. We have more entertainment, more distractions, and more social connectivity than ever before—yet mental health issues have skyrocketed. It tells us that external factors alone do not bring lasting Inner peace. Instead, our ability to process emotions, the quality of our relationships, and our mindset play a crucial role.

## Why Inner Peace is Not About External Achievements but Inner Peace

Society often conditions us to believe that Inner Peace is discovered in professional success, wealth, or social status. This belief creates what psychologists call the **Hedonic Treadmill**, where people constantly chase achievements only to find that each milestone brings temporary satisfaction before they seek the next goal.

Research in neuroscience shows that the **dopamine system**, responsible for pleasure and reward, spikes when we accomplish a goal but quickly returns to baseline. That means external rewards rarely provide lasting contentment, no matter how significant. On the other hand, practices we will discuss in this book are saying sorry, seeking forgiveness, gratitude, and love, ** have been shown to create **long-term inner peace by rewiring neural pathways instead of chasing Inner Peace externally, focusing on emotional resilience, self-awareness, and human connection offers a path to **sustainable well-being.**

## The Importance of Self-Awareness and Emotional Intelligence in Inner Peace

Emotional intelligence (EQ) is our ability to understand, regulate, and express emotions effectively. Studies show that people with high EQ experience greater overall happiness and success than those with a high IQ but low EQ.**

Self-awareness is an important component of emotional intelligence. It enables us to:

- Develop more effective coping strategies

- Enhance relationships through empathy and understanding

- Make better decisions and reduce impulsive reactions

Identify our emotional triggers

The **Four Pillars of Inner Peace**

—Saying Sorry,

—Forgiveness,

—Gratitude, and

—Love

is deeply connected to emotional intelligence. These practices allow us to navigate complex emotions, improve relationships, and develop a sense of peace and fulfillment.

## The Four Pillars: Enduring Wisdom Across Cultures and Philosophies

Throughout time, religions, various cultures, and philosophies have underscored similar principles for attaining a fulfilled life:

- **Buddhism** Promotes compassion, gratitude, and forgiveness as pathways to enlightenment.

- **Stoicism** Advocates for emotional control and gratitude as mechanisms for building resilience.

- **Christianity & Islam** Emphasize the significance of love, forgiveness, and gratitude in spiritual development.

- **Hinduism also emphasizes love (Prema/Bhakti), forgiveness (Kshama), and gratitude (Kruta-jñata) as essential for spiritual growth

- **Modern Psychology** Validates that mindfulness, gratitude, and emotional regulation enhance mental health and well-being.

These shared teachings emphasize the enduring impact of forgiveness, gratitude, and love on fostering a meaningful and fulfilling life.

## Scientific Evidence: How These Four Actions Impact Brain Chemistry

Each of the Four Pillars of Inner Peace directly influences brain chemistry and mental health:

1. **Saying Sorry** - Lowers cortisol (the stress hormone), reduces emotional tension, and fosters healthier relationships.

2. **Forgiveness** - Activates brain areas linked to emotional regulation, reducing anxiety and resentment.

3. **Practicing Gratitude** - Increases serotonin and dopamine levels, which enhance mood and mental resilience.

4. **Love** - Releases oxytocin, known as the "bonding hormone," promoting feelings of connection and security.

Research from neuroscience and psychology supports the idea that **Saying Sorry **forgiveness, gratitude, and love are key to

psychological and physical well-being.** MRI studies have shown that people who regularly practice gratitude and forgiveness have stronger neural pathways linked to positive feelings and reduced levels of stress-related brain activity.

**The Goal of This Book: A Practical Guide to Lasting Inner Peace**

This book is designed as a practical guide to implementing the Four Pillars of Inner Peace in daily life.
Each section explores one pillar in-depth, providing:
- **Scientific evidence** supporting its benefits
- **Real-life examples** illustrating its impact
- **Step-by-step exercises** to help cultivate these habits
By the end of this book, you will have the

tools to achieve **lasting inner peace** through simple yet profound life changes.

True inner peace is not found in wealth, status, or possessions but in the **way we think, feel, and connect with others.**

Welcome to your journey toward **a Peaceful, Happier, more Fulfilling life.** Let's

begin.

# PART 1:

# SAYING SORRY- THE POWER OF APOLOGY

## Why Saying Sorry Matters

"Please accept my apologies." These are essential words that convey tremendous weight. Eventually, we have all been on both sides of this situation — either saying 'sorry' or waiting for an apology. Be that as it may, have you imagined why a few expressions of remorse feel profoundly mending while others crash and burn? Why does saying sorry matter so much, and why does it feel so difficult to do it do?

It's more than words; an apology bridges conflict and resolution, pain and healing. A genuine statement of regret does ponder reconstructing trust, fixing connections, and, on occasion, in any event, evolving lives. However, a poorly delivered or insincere apology can have the exact opposite effect—widening the gap and leaving emotional wounds open and unresolved.

# CHAPTER 1:

# The Psychology of an Apology

**What Makes an Apology Meaningful?**

A meaningful apology is about being sincere and showing understanding. It includes three main parts:

**Sincerity**

An apology should come from the heart. It won't have much effect if you apologize just to move on. Being sincere means being present and open about your feelings.

Example: If a friend accidentally spills coffee on your favorite sweater, a quick, dismissive "Sorry" while they're on their phone won't feel genuine. Instead, if they look you in the eye and say, "I'm sorry. I understand how much that sweater means to you. How can I fix this?" it feels more real.

**Understanding**

A true apology shows that you understand the pain you might have caused. It requires putting yourself in the other person's shoes and recognizing their feelings.

**Timing**

When you apologize matters. If you apologize too soon, it may seem rushed. If you wait too long, it might feel like you don't care. The best time to apologize is when emotions have calmed down enough for both sides to talk openly.

## The Psychological Impact of an Apology

### For the Provider

Saying 'sorry' isn't just about fixing a relationship; it's likewise an opportunity to develop personally. It requires true humility and courage to acknowledge your mistakes and fully take responsibility for them. While this can be an intense and awkward cycle, it frequently brings a positive feeling and individual freedom.

On a psychological level, genuinely expressing regret can help ease feelings of guilt and restore your self-esteem. Studies indicate that expressing sorrow activates the brain's reward system, producing pleasurable chemicals such as dopamine. As a result, people often express feeling "lighter" or truly relieved after delivering a sincere apology.

For the Recipient

The effect of a sincere conciliatory sentiment on the beneficiary can be similarly critical. It approves of their feelings, recognizes their aggravation, and shows that their experience genuinely matters. A genuine expression of remorse likewise flags that substantial steps are being taken to make things right. This is often the most important step towards personal healing.

A clever display of regret can have the opposite effect. Instead of resolving the problem, it can develop wounds and support questions. It's like covering a wound without first sanitizing it — the underlying harm continues to fester and degrade over time.

Contextual analyses:

Toyota's Corporate Expression of Remorse

During the audit crisis of 2009-2010, Toyota faced public backlash over security issues that led to various concerns incidents. In like manner, the association's chief, Akio Toyoda, delivered an overall affirmation, which was conveyed around the world. His significant and sad area focused on Toyota's commitment to client security. Despite starting an examination of the association's lazy response, Toyoda's genuine conciliatory viewpoint restored confidence and rehabilitated the image of its brand.

## Conclusion: The Power of Apologies to Transform Relationships

A genuine expression of remorse is one of the most amazing assets for fixing and reinforcing connections. It requires weakness, fortitude, and empathy, yet the prizes are unlimited. When executed properly, an apology not only heals the person receiving it but also transforms the one delivering it.

So the following time you end up wondering whether or not to say those two little words, recall this: the fortitude to apologize is certainly not an indication of shortcoming — it's an indication of solidarity and development. Also, in those snapshots of weakness, you have the ability to transform struggle into association and agony into progress.

# Chapter 2: The Science of Regret and Guilt

## The Weight of Regret and Guilt

Guilt and regret are general human encounters. Sooner or later, we as a whole end up wishing we had gone with various decisions or acted diversely in specific circumstances. These sentiments can torment us. However, they additionally hold groundbreaking power when perceived and tended to.

In this section, we'll investigate the science behind Guilt and Regret, checking out their underlying foundations in the Brain and their effect on emotional wellness. By understanding these feelings, we can figure out how to oversee them and try not to fall into the trap of toxic shame.

## The Neuroscience of Regret and Guilt

Regret and guilt are often combined together, but they originate from slightly different processes in the brain. Regret is usually connected to decisions or actions that didn't lead to the desired outcome, while guilt revolves around feeling responsible for the harm caused to others.

### The Brain and Regret

Regret primarily activates the orbitofrontal cortex (OFC), a region of the brain involved in decision-making and evaluating outcomes. This part of the brain enables us to reflect on the past and imagine various scenarios. That's why you can't help but replay that one awkward moment or poor decision in your mind—

your brain is literally wired to evaluate what might have been.

The Brain and Guilt

Guilt engages the anterior cingulate cortex (ACC) and amygdala, regions associated with empathy and emotional processing. When we feel guilty, these areas work together to generate the physical discomfort and emotional heaviness often associated with guilt.

This discomfort serves a social function designed to motivate us to repair relationships and restore balance.

Fun Fact: Studies using MRI scans show that people who frequently experience guilt have stronger connections between their ACC and empathy centers in the brain, suggesting that guilt-prone individuals may naturally have a better understanding of the feelings of others.

## Constructive Guilt vs. Toxic Shame

While guilt can be a constructive emotion that helps us acknowledge mistakes and seek forgiveness, it's important to differentiate it from toxic shame. Understanding the distinction is key to maintaining healthy emotional well-being.

### Constructive Guilt

Useful responsibility is explicit and noteworthy. It's associated with a particular occasion or conduct and spurs us to set things right. For instance:

Situation: You missed a significant gathering and feel regretful for letting your group down.

Activity: Apologize to your colleagues and resolve issues more efficiently and effectively. Embracing helpful responsibilities serves as an ethical compass, guiding us toward becoming better versions of ourselves.

## Toxic Shame

Toxic shame, on the other hand, is pervasive and connected to our identity rather than our actions. It's the voice in your head that says, "I'm a bad person," instead of "I made a bad choice." This pessimistic mentality can prompt sensations of uselessness and Self-hate

Example: A child who grows up in an environment where mistakes are severely punished may develop a shame-based mindset, believing they're intrinsically flawed rather than recognizing their mistakes as learning opportunities.

.

## The Effect of Unsettled Guilt/Regret on Psychological Well-Being

When guilt or regret are left unresolved, they can negatively impact mental health, resulting in feelings of anxiety, sadness, and, unexpectedly, physical symptoms. Here are a few ways unresolved guilt affects us:

## Rumination

Guilt and regret often lead to overthinking and replaying past mistakes. This rumination can trap one in a cycle of regret and self-blame, preventing one from moving forward.

## Anxiety and Depression

Chronic guilt/Regret can contribute to feelings of hopelessness and being overwhelmed, which are common symptoms of depression. It can also increase anxiety, as you continually fear making future mistakes.

## Physical Symptoms

Guilt /Regret doesn't just affect your mind—it affects your body too. Persistent guilt has been linked to increased stress, headaches, and even digestive issues.

## Conclusion.Embracing Development in Guilt and Regret

Regret and guilt, though uncomfortable, are strong educators. They shine a light on our characteristics and allow us to create. By understanding the science behind these sentiments and sorting out some way to supervise them beneficially, we can change depictions of distress into catalysts for change.

Whenever you're burdened by Guilt, recollect: it's not necessary to focus on deleting the past but on gaining from it. Regret is definitely not an impasse — it fills in as an establishment for a more promising time to come.

# Chapter 3:

# Why People Struggle to Apologize

## The Challenge of Saying "I'm Sorry"

Why is saying sorry so difficult? If saying "I'm sorry" can repair relationships and ease tensions, why do so many people avoid it? The answer lies in the complex interplay of human psychology, social conditioning, and cultural influences. This chapter will explore the barriers to apologizing, including ego, fear of vulnerability, and societal norms. By understanding these challenges, we can learn how to overcome them and make the act of apologizing more accessible and easier.

### The Role of Ego and Pride

At the heart of many struggles to apologize is the ego. Apologizing requires us to admit that we made a mistake, which can feel like an attack on our self-image. For some, this recognition of wrongdoing is viewed as a sign of weakness or failure.

**Why Ego Gets in the Way**:

Self-Security:

The main function of our self-image is to protect our sense of worth. Admitting an error might expose a weakness, which could make us open to criticism or rejection..

Anxiety toward Losing Status:

Expressions of regret can feel like a shift in power. Some individuals emphasize that admitting to problems may make them appear sub-par or less competent, particularly in professional or diverse settings.

Perfectionism:

Individuals with perfectionist tendencies may find it challenging to acknowledge mistakes because they've linked their self-worth to an image of flawlessness

Example: A manager may hesitate to apologize to their team, fearing it will undermine their authority. Ironically, a true apology often strengthens respect and trust.

Fear of Vulnerability

Apologizing is an inherently vulnerable act. It requires opening up to the possibility of rejection, anger, or a lack of forgiveness.

This fear may hinder individuals from initiating reconciliation.

Common Vulnerability Fears:

Dismissal:

"Consider the possibility that they don't acknowledge my expression of remorse."

Concerns about being dismissed may lead people to refrain from apologizing, preferring to sidestep the matter rather than face potential emotional discomfort.

Profound Openness:

Saying sorry reflects an admission of accountability, which may evoke feelings of shame or inadequacy. This level of vulnerability can be daunting.

Vulnerability:

Saying 'sorry' demonstrates an affirmation of responsibility, which might bring out sensations of disgrace or insufficiency. This degree of weakness can plague.

Social and Cultural Factors

Social and cultural norms significantly affect how people view and approach apologies. In some cultures, apologizing is seen as a sign of respect and honor; in others, it may be viewed as a loss of face or status.

Cultural Influences on Apologies:

Collectivist versus Individualist Cultures:

In collectivist cultures (e.g., Japan and Korea), apologizing is often seen as a way to maintain harmony and show respect. Public apologies are common and expected.

In individualist cultures (e.g., the U.S.), apologizing can sometimes be seen as a personal defeat or a sign of weakness.

Gender Norms:

Studies show that women are generally more likely to apologize than men, partly due to social conditioning. Women are often taught to prioritize relationships and harmony, while men may be conditioned to see apologies as a threat to their authority.

Family Dynamics:

Early experiences shape our views on apologies. A child raised in a household where mistakes were punished harshly might develop a connection between apologies and feelings of shame, leading to hesitance in expressing remorse as an adult.

## Psychological Resistance to Apologizing

### Cognitive Dissonance

People want to see themselves as good individuals. When we hurt someone, this view of ourselves clashes with our actions, creating cognitive dissonance. Rather than admitting fault, many people justify their acts to protect their self-concept.

Example: Someone who cancels plans at the last minute might think, "I'm not unreliable; I was just too busy," rather than apologizing for the inconvenience.

## Fear of Escalation

Some people avoid apologizing because they fear it will lead to further conflict. They may worry that admitting fault will invite criticism or confrontation.

## Conclusion: Embracing the Courage to Apologize

Apologizing is rarely easy, but it is always worthwhile. By understanding the psychological and social barriers that make apologies challenging, we can start to dismantle them and approach conflict resolution with greater confidence. Apologies are acts of bravery that require us to set aside our pride, embrace vulnerability, and prioritize connection over ego.

When you feel resistance to apologizing, ask yourself: What's truly at stake—my pride or my relationships? In most cases, the courage to say "I'm sorry" is the first step toward healing and growth for you and the people around you.

# Chapter 4:

# The Art of a Genuine Apology

## Apologizing Is a Skill

Saying "I'm sorry" may sound simple, but crafting a genuine apology is an art. It's not just about uttering words of regret; it's about showing true accountability, empathy, and a willingness to make amends. This chapter explores the elements that make an apology genuine, the pitfalls to avoid, and examples of apologies from different contexts—personal relationships, business, and leadership.

### The 5 Elements of an Effective Apology

What separates a genuine apology from a hollow one? Here are the five key elements that make an apology impactful:

#### Acknowledgment of Harm

Clearly state what you did wrong. A vague or incomplete acknowledgment can make the apology feel insincere.

Example: Instead of saying, "I'm sorry if I upset you," say, "I'm sorry for interrupting you during your presentation. I realize it was disrespectful and disruptive."

Empathy and Understanding

Show that you understand how your actions affected the other person. Use phrases like, "I can see how this hurt you" or "I understand why this made you feel frustrated."

Genuine Regret

Express your remorse sincerely. Avoid excuses or justifications that shift the blame.

Example: "I regret not prioritizing our meeting. It was wrong of me to let you down."

### Commitment to Change

Offer a plan to ensure the mistake won't happen again. Actions often speak louder than words.

Example: "In the future, I'll set reminders to ensure I'm on time."

### Reparation

If possible, ask how you can make things right. This demonstrates your commitment to repairing the harm.

Example: "Can I do anything to make up for this?

Common Mistakes When Apologizing

Even with the best intentions, many apologies fall flat because of these common pitfalls:

Using Conditional Language

Saying, "I'm sorry if I offended you," places doubt on the other person's feelings and shifts responsibility away from you. Avoid "if" or "but" in your apology.

Making It About Yourself

Focus on the other person's experience rather than your own feelings. "I feel so bad about this" shifts the attention to you instead of validating the other person's emotions.

Overexplaining or Justifying

Providing too much context can sound like an excuse. Stick to taking responsibility for your actions.

Rushing the Apology

A hasty apology can seem insincere. Take the time to reflect on your actions before apologizing.

# Chapter 5:

# Practical Exercises on Saying Sorry

## Turning Knowledge into Action

Understanding the theory behind apologies is important, but real growth occurs when we put it into practice. Effectively apologizing requires self-awareness, empathy, and practice. This chapter offers practical exercises to help you develop the skills necessary for crafting genuine apologies, whether in personal relationships, professional settings, or even with others yourself.

Exercise 1: Guided Journaling for Self-Reflection

Journaling is a powerful tool for self-reflection. Use the following prompts to explore past conflicts and your approach to apologies:

Identify a Past Context Conflict:

Describe a situation where you hurt someone or made a mistake. What happened, and how did you handle it?

Reflect on Your Emotions:

What emotions did you feel at the time? Did you experience feelings of defensiveness, guilt, or shame?

Analyze the Outcome:

Was the issue resolved? If it wasn't, what could you have done differently?

Plan for the Future Apologies:

Write a hypothetical apology for the situation. Include acknowledgment of harm, genuine regret, and a commitment to change.

Tip: Revisit your journal regularly to monitor your progress and recognize patterns in your behavior.

Exercise 2: The Apology Formula Practice

Use this formula to craft an effective apology:

State What You're Apologizing For:

Be specific. Avoid vague or generic statements.

Example: I'm sorry for not returning your call when you needed support.

Acknowledge the Impact:

Demonstrate empathy by addressing how your actions affected the other person.

Example: I understand that my silence made you feel abandoned and unimportant.

Express Genuine Regret:

Show that you're genuinely sorry without making excuses.

Example: I regret not being there for you and feel terrible about letting you down.

Commit to Change:

Outline the steps you'll take to avoid repeating the mistake.

Example: I'll respond promptly in the future, especially when you need me.

Practice: Write three apologies for different scenarios—a personal relationship, a professional conflict, and a minor everyday mistake. Review them to ensure they follow the formula.

Exercise 3: Role-Playing Apologies

Role-playing allows you to practice apologizing in a safe and controlled environment. Follow these steps:

Choose a Scenario:

Pick a real-life situation or create a hypothetical one. For example, apologizing to a friend for missing their birthday party.

Partner Up:

Ask a trusted friend, family member, or colleague to act as the other party in the scenario. If that's not possible, practice in front of a mirror.

Deliver Your Apology:

Use the apology formula to craft and deliver your message.

Receive Feedback:

Ask your partner for tone, body language, and sincerity feedback.

Advanced Challenge: Practice responding to different reactions, such as forgiveness, anger, or rejection, to build resilience and adaptability.

Exercise 4: The 30-Day Apology Challenge

Commit to a 30-day challenge to build your apology skills. Each week focuses on a different aspect:

Week 1: Self-Awareness

Identify situations where you've hurt others but haven't apologized. Write a list and reflect on why you avoided apologizing.

Week 2: Low-Stakes Apologies

Start with minor conflicts, such as accidentally interrupting someone or forgetting to respond to a text—practice using the apology formula.

Week 3: Difficult Apologies

Tackle more significant unresolved issues. Take time to prepare and deliver thoughtful apologies.

Week 4: Apologizing to Yourself

Reflect on moments of self-blame. Write yourself an apology letter, acknowledging your humanity and committing to self-compassion.

Goal: By the end of the 30 days, you'll have a deeper understanding of apology dynamics and greater confidence in your ability to say sorry effectively.

Exercise 5: Body Language Awareness

Body language plays a crucial role in how an apology is received. Practice the following:

Maintain Eye Contact:

Look the other person in the eye to convey sincerity.

Use Open Gestures:

Avoid crossing your arms or appearing defensive. Use open, relaxed gestures to show you're approachable.

Watch Your Tone:

Speak calmly, and avoid rushing. A genuine tone can make or break your apology.

Tip: Record yourself delivering an apology and analyze your body language. Adjust as needed to ensure your nonverbal cues align with your words.

Exercise 6: Apology Scripts for Common Situations

Here are templates for common apology scenarios. Customize them to fit your situation:

For Forgetting an Important Date:

I'm sorry I forgot your birthday. I know how much it meant to you, and I regret not being more thoughtful. I want to make it up to you by planning a special day together.

For Professional Oversight:

I apologize for missing the project deadline. I understand this caused inconvenience for the team. I've adjusted my workflow to ensure it doesn't happen again and am committed to making up for the delay.

For a Misunderstanding in a Relationship:

I'm sorry for how I responded earlier. I realize my words were dismissive, which wasn't my intention. I value our relationship and want to ensure I listen better moving forward.

Practice:

Write your scripts for scenarios you've encountered recently. Deliver them to a friend or practice aloud.

## Conclusion: Building the Habit of Apologizing

Apologizing is a skill that requires practice and intentionality. Engaging in these exercises will improve your ability to apologize, strengthen your relationships, and deepen your understanding of yourself. Remember, the courage to say "I'm sorry" is a gift you give to others and yourself—fostering growth, healing, and connection.

# PART 2:

# FORGIVENESS – LETTING GO OF RESENTMENT

# Chapter6: Understanding Forgiveness

## Defining Forgiveness

Forgiving others is one of an individual's most profound acts, yet it is commonly misinterpreted. Lots of people see forgiveness as an approval of unsafe habits or an indication of a weak point. Actually, it has to do with reclaiming your tranquility and releasing animosity instead of justifying the misdoings done to you. This chapter examines the true meaning of forgiveness, the role of empathy in the process, and how various spiritual and philosophical perspectives have influenced our understanding

## What Forgiveness Is—and What It Isn't

Let's begin by clarifying what forgiveness involves and dispelling common myths surrounding it:

**What Forgiveness Is**:

<u>A Choice to Release Resentment</u>: It includes the choice to release temper or resentment toward those that have triggered your discomfort.

<u>A Path to Inner Peace</u>: Forgiving one more individual primarily profits the forgiver, aiding to minimize the psychological weight of previous experiences.

<u>An Act of Strength</u>: Forgiving encourages you to handle your feelings and protects against previous misdoings from specifying your future

**What Forgiveness Isn't:**

Condoning Misconduct: Forgiveness does not indicate that you settle on or belittle the misdoings done to you.

Forgetting the Past: It does not imply getting rid of uncomfortable memories; instead, you can change your point of view on those memories so they no longer control your life.

Reconciliation: Forgiveness plus settlement are unique; you can forgive somebody without desiring to bring back the partnership, particularly if it is undesirable or hazardous.

## The Importance of Empathy in Forgiveness

Empathy plays a crucial role in forgiveness, as it involves recognizing the humanity in others without excusing their actions.

**Relevance of compassion in forgiveness**:

Acquiring Perspective: Understanding that others might act out of their very own discomfort can move your sight from animosity to concern.

Humanizing the Offender: Considering an offender's struggles makes it easier to separate their actions from their worth as individuals.

<u>Concentrating on Yourself</u>: Prioritizing your feelings plus recognizing your discomfort is essential for recovery.

For example, if someone cuts you off in traffic, a lack of compassion might lead to anger, while compassion could help you consider that they might be rushing due to an emergency or simply making a mistake.

**Religious and Philosophical Views on Forgiveness**

Forgiveness has been a central theme in numerous religious and philosophical teachings throughout history. Here are a few perspectives:

Christianity is central to Christian beliefs. Jesus's words, "Forgive them, for they know not what they do," emphasize the importance of forgiveness, even in severe suffering.

Buddhism teaches that forgiveness involves releasing anger and resentment, which enables you to break free from the cycle of suffering. The concept of "metta" (loving-kindness) nurtures compassion for all, even for those who have harmed you.

In Islam, forgiveness is seen as a divine quality. The Quran often emphasizes Allah's mercy, encouraging believers to embody this by forgiving others, which promotes spiritual tranquility.

Secular Philosophy: Thinkers like Friedrich Nietzsche viewed forgiveness as a transformative act that liberates individuals from resentment. Modern psychology sees it as a tool for personal empowerment and emotional well-being rather than merely a moral duty.

**Study: The Power of Forgiveness**

Take the instance of Nelson Mandela, who, after spending 27 years behind bars throughout South Africa's apartheid, chose forgiveness instead of revenge upon his release. His choice to let go of bitterness helped unify South Africa and promote healing. Mandela's story highlights that forgiveness is an individual act and a significant catalyst for societal transformation.

## Conclusion: Forgiveness as Freedom

Forgiveness is not centered around the individual who caused you pain; it's primarily about you. It's a gift you offer yourself—an opportunity to release your emotional weight and regain tranquility. By grasping the essence of forgiveness, nurturing compassion, and contemplating the insights of age-old wisdom, you can start to view forgiveness as a journey toward liberation and recovery. The next chapter will explore how forgiveness affects the brain and body, revealing the science behind this transformative process.

# Chapter 7:

# The Neuroscience of Forgiveness

## Forgiveness and the Brain.

Forgiveness is not merely an act of the mind. When we forgive, it has a profound impact on both mind and body. It releases the anger we previously held, allowing us to reduce stress and positively influence our health overall. This chapter looks at the effect forgiveness has on the brain and its ability to reduce stress levels and change lives.

## How Forgiveness Changes Brain Activity

When we hold onto anger, bitterness, and resentment, we activate certain areas of our brain, keeping that part highly active and keeping us in a stress mode. Forgiveness, however, reverses this situation, calming these areas and bringing them down while rewarding others and turning on more of our empathy centers and other aspects promoting peace.

**The Secret Areas of the Mind Include**:

**Amygdala (Threat detector)** –

It is responsible for emotions like anxiety and anger. When we think about the traumatic things people have done to us, that part of the brain might become overactive, allowing the body to remain in a state of tension or anxiousness. Forgiveness reduces activity in the amygdala and lets the brain know that a threat has passed. Prefrontal Cortex (The Rational Thinker) -.

**The prefrontal cortex** —

The part of the brain that helps us make decisions and practice compassion goes to work, helping to regulate our emotions better and look at things differently.

**Anterior Cingulate Cortex (The Conflict Resolver)**:

This region is related to regulating emotional distress and problem-resolving. Studies demonstrate that when one grants forgiveness, the anterior cingulate cortex becomes activated, cultivating an understanding of a feeling of empathy toward the offender.

Brain scans suggest that when people experience forgiveness, the prefrontal cortex is more active, and the amygdala decreases. This suggests that forgiving others helps shift the mind from quick emotional reactions to more thoughtful thinking.

**How Forgiveness Reduces Stress:**

Lower Cortisol Levels: Cortisol is the body's primary stress hormone and accounts for chronic stress, depression, and mental illness. Anger and resentment trigger cortisol release. Forgiveness stems cortisol production and increases blood flow through vital organs, significantly restoring the body to homeostasis.

**Enhance Cardiovascular Health**:

Chronic anxiety can lead to elevated BP and pressure, which increases the risk of cardiovascular diseases. Research suggests that forgiveness reduces high blood pressure and improves heart health.

Boosts Immune Function: Chronic anxiety weakens the body's immune system, making us more vulnerable to illness. Forgiveness has been linked to better immune responses, allowing the body to fight off infections and heal faster.

In one study at Stanford University, individuals who were trained to practice forgiveness experienced reductions in anxiety and exhibited a decrease in their symptoms of physical distress, including headaches and fatigue.

**Study**: Those Who Forgave and Experienced Transformation Eva Kor's Story Holocaust survivor Eva Kor endured the unthinkable in Auschwitz. Decades after she was liberated, she offered her forgiveness to the Nazi doctor who experimented on her and her twin sister.

Kor said forgiveness was a “gift" to herself, one that released her from the “pain" of her “own inner rage and hatred." Her story exemplifies the profound emotional and physical transformation that can result from forgiving.

## Conclusion: Forgiveness as a Brain and Body Booster

Forgiveness is not simply an emotional or spiritual practice but also a neurological and physiological one. By releasing resentment, we reduce the overactivity of the threat centers in our brains, diminish the hormones of stress, and allow empathy and peace to emerge. Science is now proving that forgiveness is transformative of the mind and healing for the body. The next chapter will examine the cost of holding grudges and how one can step off of this kind of karmic cycle and release resentment.

# CHAPTER 8:

# THE COST OF HOLDING ONTO GRUDGES

Although you may feel that holding onto a grudge protects you from being hurt again, you are causing more damage to yourself than to the person who hurt you. Resentment can cling to us, weighing heavily on our mental and physical well-being. In this chapter, we will explore how holding onto grudges affects your mind and body, how unresolved anger contributes to mental health issues, and helpful ways to free yourself from the blame game.

## Mental Effects of Holding onto Grudges

Nursing a grudge can keep you awake at night and drain your energy during the day, consuming all of your mental space. When you cling to a grudge, you struggle to release the bitterness and anger that stem from the experience. Your mind stays fixated on the event, replaying it endlessly, reopening old wounds and hindering your ability to heal.

**How Grudges Affect Your Mental State**

You're Constantly Reflecting "Thinking about what happened over and over—whether with colleagues at work, friends at brunch, or even in your own mind—feels really good," said Michael Poulin, PhD, an associate professor of psychology at the State University of New York in Buffalo. "When someone else validates your anger, or when you're dwelling on it alone, it can feel really good." However, constant rumination actually strengthens those negative emotions. The more you process the painful event, the more stressful and anxiety-inducing it becomes. That friend who insulted you at the party may not have meant to offend you, but every time you revisit the argument, you feel just as hurt as you did in the moment

Relationship Damage:

Holding a grudge builds an emotional barrier, making it hard to interact with people. You run the risk of becoming too guarded or wary, and this can affect relationships with people who aren't those who hurt you in the first place, HuffPost UK Lifestyle notes.

Drains Emotional Energy:

Resentment can drain your emotional energy, leaving you with less capacity for joy, creativity, and other positive experiences.

Insight: Research shows those who cling to grudges suffer from depression and low self-esteem and find it harder to manage anger. Your body on grudges Resentment is more than a nasty chip on your shoulder; it also has a physical presence. Carrying around a grudge can weigh you down with tension, and that strain compounds over the weeks, months, and, if nursed for too long, years, it stays with you. Here's what holding a grudge can do to your body: Flood it with stress hormones. Staying mad keeps your body in a state of constant alertness, causing it to release stress hormones like cortisol. Flooding your system with cortisol on an extended basis can weaken your immune system and raise your risk of heart disease.

Heightened Cardiovascular Risks:

Research has linked resentment and anger with increased blood pressure, heart disease, and strokes. Scientists associate these heightened risks with the greater levels of stress that come with holding onto a grudge. Fitful, low-quality sleep: Resentment often causes restless nights. Unresolved conflicts and disagreements in your mind make it difficult to get the quality of rest that you need.

Digestive Problems:

Chronic stress can throw off the gut-brain connection, sometimes leading to gastrointestinal conditions such as irritable bowel syndrome (IBS).

For example, a research study published in the journal *Emotion* found that people who forgive, as opposed to those who harbor anger, have lower blood pressure and fewer physical symptoms.

Unprocessed anger doesn't simply disappear. It can morph into other mental health conditions, such as depression and anxiety.

## The Link Between Anger and Mental Health:

Depression: Anger that you don't express is called repressed anger. Often, this turns inward. You may take the blame for things or start feeling hopeless or worthless. For example, someone who can't stop thinking about a betrayal may begin to feel that they don't deserve love or loyalty.

Anxiety:

Living in a state of resentment often leaves you dreading future pain. That ongoing sense of watchfulness and wariness can easily morph into anxiety, which makes it difficult to relax.

Emotional triggers:

Resentment may cause overreactions to seemingly minor indignities, turning small disputes into enormous wells of emotional energy.

Insight:

Unresolved anger changes how your brain is wired, making you expect conflict and danger. Ultimately, it makes future stressors and distrust easier for us to anticipate and process (even when it isn't helpful).

**Study**: Getting Rid Of Animosity James's Experience: James's successful company owner brought a grudge against his organization companion for several years after a befall that finished their collaboration. The animosity impacted his capacity to rely on brand-new partners and also added to regular migraine headaches plus sleep problems. With treatment, James discovered reframe the dishonesty as a beneficial lesson in establishing borders. By forgiving his ex-partner, she discovered tranquility and also reconstructed his self-confidence, ultimately beginning a flourishing brand-new company.

## Final Thoughts: Letting Go to Move On

Animosities may appear to be a form of self-protection; however, at some point, they become self-destructive. Animosity keeps you trapped in past discomfort, preventing you from fully experiencing the present. By recognizing the toll animosities take on your psychological and physical well-being and committing to overcome them, you can regain your psychological freedom and enhance your overall well-being.

# Chapter 9:

# The Four Levels of Forgiveness

**Forgiveness Doesn't Look The Same For Everyone**

Forgiveness is often viewed as a one-time event. The reality is much more complex. Not every incident is created (or forgiven) equally, and the level of forgiveness needed will vary based on the type of event you encounter. In this chapter, we will explore the four levels of forgiveness: Each one requires a distinct mindset and tools, and we will provide specific, action-oriented strategies for navigating through it.

## Forgiving a Minor Offense

Petty offenses are the small grievances of daily life that can easily pile up if not dealt with. Examples include that friend who cancels plans at the last minute or the coworker who steals the spotlight for a minor idea. These incidents might not have heavy impacts, but they can lead to unfavorable relations if unresolved.

Steps to Forgive a Minor Offense:

Acknowledge Your Feelings: Recognize that you feel irritated or hurt by this person's slight against you, no matter how small. It is important to admit this to yourself. If you write it off or try to ignore it, you could build up resentment over time.

Consider Intentions:

Take into account whether the rule breaker did so intentionally or accidentally. More often than not, minor rule breakers do so out of carelessness rather than malice.

Talk It Out (If You Need To):

Sometimes, a simple, direct conversation can smooth things over if the offense was minor. For instance, "I was disappointed when you canceled on such short notice. Can you give me more of a heads-up next time?"

Let It Go. Once you air your grievance, make a conscious choice to let it go. Remind yourself that clinging to petty grievances isn't worth it.

Forgive a friend for failing to return a borrowed book by telling yourself, "Oh, that was an oversight on their part rather than a personal affront to me."

## 2. Forgiving Deep Betrayals

Deep betrayals, such as infidelity, broken trust, or abandonment, require a far more complex process. These wounds can leave lasting scars and may take years to heal fully.

Steps to Forgive Deep Betrayals:

1. Allow Yourself to Feel. Don't rush the process. Sitting with your emotions and processing the pain before moving toward forgiveness is important.

Understand the Context:

Although understanding doesn't condone the behavior, it can help you understand the betrayal. Was it motivated by fear, insecurity, or some other underlying issue?

Set Boundaries:

Forgiveness doesn't mean allowing the same behavior to repeat. Set clear boundaries to protect yourself in the future.

Seek support:

Working with a therapist or trusted confidant will help you work through the emotional experience of deep betrayals.

Take Your Time:

Forgiving such deep wounds takes time. Be patient with yourself and honor your journey.

Example: A spouse forgives his partner for infidelity after months of counseling, open dialogue, and mutually agreed upon methods for rebuilding the trust in the relationship.

## 3. Forgiving Yourself

Forgiving yourself is often the most difficult level of forgiveness. Whether it's a past mistake, an opportunity missed, or something harmful you did to someone else, it requires deep soul work.

Steps to Forgive Yourself:

Acknowledge your mistakes:

Accept that you have made a mistake, and take responsibility for your actions without getting into a self-blame cycle. Instead of saying, "I made a mistake," use phrases like "I am a mistake."

Reflect on growth:

How has this experience changed you or taught you? How have you learned and grown as a person? Only through our mistakes can we grow as individuals.

Practice self-compassion:

Treat yourself as kindly as you would your best friend. Remind yourself that everyone makes mistakes.

Make amends (when possible):

If your past actions hurt others, apologize and make it right. This not only makes others feel better, but it can also help you feel better.

Release Yourself from Perfectionist Impossible Standards:

Recognize that you will keep making mistakes because you are human. Remember that forgiveness is a practice, not a destination.

Exercise:

Write a letter to yourself, admitting your mistake, explaining how and why it happened, and vowing to move on with a sense of compassion.

**4. Radical Forgiveness**

Radical forgiveness moves beyond individual acts of forgiving and paradigms. Practicing radical forgiveness is akin to embracing an outlook on life rather than simply going through acts of forgiveness. Spiritual or philosophical level Often involves transformative experiences and healing from heavy or even deep trauma.

Principles of Radical Forgiveness

Reframe Your Thoughts:

Look at the offense in a new way. Consider it as an opportunity for growth and transformation. Ask yourself, "What can I learn from this experience?" Look at the big picture: Understand that everyone is on their own journey, and act the way they do because of their unique life experiences and struggles to help you develop compassion for those who hurt you.

Let Go of the Need to Be Right:

Release the desire for revenge. Radical forgiveness is all about letting go of your own burden.

Connect to something greater:

For some people, radical forgiveness is deeply rooted in a sense of spirituality or connection to others. "Prayer, mindfulness or meditation, or even just going into nature can be helpful practices," Susic said.

**Conclusion: Choosing the Right Level**

Forgiveness is ultimately an individual decision. There is no one answer for everyone. Depending on the degree of offense and your own willingness to forgive, different levels of forgiveness will apply. Whether you are forgiving a relatively harmless comment on your hairstyle, working with someone who has cheated on you, or forgiving yourself, forgiveness in any way is liberating. Next, we will look at what to do when you feel forgiveness is impossible. You will find ideas for managing even the most difficult of situations.

# Chapter 10:

# How to Forgive When It Feels Impossible

## The Unforgivable Feels Overwhelming

There are times when forgiving feels impossible. Maybe the people who cultivated the hurt continue to betray you. Perhaps they abused you for so long that forgiveness feels like a betrayal of yourself. Or maybe the wound forged in your heart is so intense, so life-altering, you always turn away from forgiving, even in your mind, because the very thought feels overwhelming. The resolution set out in the following chapter offers practical steps and emotional insight on approaching forgiveness when it feels like far too much to give. In these cases, forgiveness is not about making peace with those who have harmed you or absolving them: it's about letting go yourself to remove the toxins of the past for a clearer future.

What to Do When Someone Won't Apologize :

Forgiveness becomes even harder when the person who hurt you refuses to apologize or doesn't acknowledge their wrongdoing. In such cases, the healing process must start and end with you.

Steps to Forgive Without an Apology:
.Distinguish Forgiveness from Reconciliation: Reconciling with another is a mutual endeavor, whereas forgiveness is solely for yourself. Understand that just because you forgive someone doesn't mean you have to reconnect with them.

Validate Your Feelings:

Recognize the pain and anger you've experienced because they have been unable to apologize. Refusing to acknowledge these feelings will only lead to prolonged hurt.

Emphasize Self-Empowerment:

Remind yourself that forgiveness is about taking control of your own emotions and not allowing the offender's lack of remorse to dictate your peace.

Reframe this Situation: Instead of waiting for an apology, ask yourself: "What do I need to heal?" Redirect your energy toward self-care and personal growth.

Example: The colleague who spread false rumors about you refuses to own up to her mistakes. Rather than wallowing in a state of resentment, you concentrate on doing your best in your work and maintain a professional reputation that does your talking for you.

When it's Been Deeply Hurtful, Instances of abuse, betrayal, or loss may mark you deeply. Forgiving is a journey of courage and strength that may demand great patience, time, and cost.

Steps for Healing from Deep Suffering

Allow Yourself to Grieve: Healing begins when you recognize the magnitude of your anguish. Grieving is not a sign of weakness. It is critical to your recovery.

Seek Professional Support: A therapist or counselor can help you process trauma and develop tools for emotional healing. Therapy provides a safe space to explore your feelings and build a path toward forgiveness.

Practice self-compassion. Don't blame yourself for the hurt someone has caused you. Challenge any negative, self-blaming thoughts that you have and remind yourself that you deserve to be happy — and that you are strong and worthy.

Find Meaning in the Pain This step can seem impossible in the early stages of grieving. Though pain can feel insurmountable, many people look back on painful experiences and find meaning or lessons in them. This isn't to justify the harm they suffered—they aren't meant to suffer. But finding meaning in pain can be a guiding beacon to help them grow from the hurt.

Let Go of the Need for Justice: Waiting for others to dispense justice on your behalf only leaves you shackled to resentment. Focus instead on reclaiming your power by finding a sense of emotional closure within yourself.

Case Study: A childhood abuse survivor spends years in therapy and journaling. Slowly, they come to understand that forgiveness doesn't mean absolving their abuser of responsibility but freeing themselves of the mental prison of resentment and trauma.

Parting Ways Without an Embrace

Forgiving someone doesn't always mean letting them back in. Sometimes, it means choosing to forgive them from a distance, then moving on.

How to Forgive Without Reconnecting Set Clear Boundaries: I

f the person who hurt you is still in your life, establish boundaries to protect yourself. Boundaries are not about punishment but about creating a safe space for your well-being. Forgive for Yourself: Remind yourself that forgiveness is a gift you give to yourself. It's about unburdening your heart, not granting absolution to the offender.

Limit Emotional Triggers:

Minimize your contact with the person or with things that remind you of them. Try to create a "forgiveness-free zone"—an ecosystem of net positive people in your life. Find Closure Within: In a letter (it's okay if you never send it), express to the person how they hurt you and your decision to forgive them. This can create an internal sense of emotional resolution that helps you manage the pain and process your emotions.

An example of this is a sibling who constantly manipulates you and doesn't recognize you as a person. You can forgive them internally but choose only to see them during the holidays to preserve your peace. Tools to Help

Forgive the Impossible Forgiveness Meditation:

You can search online for a variety of guided meditations on letting go. Focus on releasing anger, bitterness, and resentment as you visualize those negative feelings floating away with every breath you exhale.

Forgiveness Journal:

Set aside a journal dedicated to your personal forgiveness journey. Record all the emotions you experience when working on forgiveness. Document the forward strides and backward steps. Celebrate every small success.

Affirmations:

“I release the past and choose peace.” ”I am strong enough to let go of resentment.” Forgiveness Journeys of Others: Read books or watch documentaries on people who have forgiven the impossible. Use their stories as road maps to lead you on your own path to healing.

## Conclusion: Forgiveness as a Personal Triumph

Forgiveness feels impossible when we're so wounded that the path to healing seems out of reach. But even in the most extreme cases, forgiveness is possible—again, not as an act of goodwill for everyone else but as your gift to yourself. By forgiving, you take your power back. You let go and make room for peace, joy, and freedom. The final chapter offers some exercises to help you deepen your practice and integrate this into your life.

# Chapter 11:

# The Science of Gratitude

## Gratitude and the Human Experience

Gratitude is more than a mere "thank you" or transient feeling; it is a profound and transformative practice that reshapes our perception of the world and interactions with others. Research demonstrates that gratitude is deeply ingrained in our biology and psychology, affecting our mental and physical health. In this chapter, we will explore how gratitude rewires our brains, is linked to happiness, and influences our physical health. By understanding the science of gratitude, we can harness its power to live fuller, richer, and more fulfilling lives.

"A different world can be made. The world becomes a warm and inviting place."

## How Gratitude Changes You and Your Brain

Activating Reward Centres –

Gratitude activates the reward centres of our brain (specifically, the ventromedial prefrontal cortex and the nucleus accumbens). Activity in these reward centres gives us pleasurable experiences through the release of dopamine (a neurotransmitter involved in pleasure). In other words, these areas are activated when we express and experience gratitude. Importantly, this makes us more inclined to experience gratitude as these areas are activated.

Gratitude boosts the release of serotonin,

Reinforcing Neural Pathways:

By noticing the positives in life with more regularity, you can strengthen the neural pathways connected to positive thinking and emotional resilience. This will make it even easier to stay more emotionally positive and focused on the good.

Rewiring the Amygdala:

Practicing gratitude reduces activity in the brain's anxiety center, the amygdala, as well as significantly reduces stress and anxiety.

For instance, research from the University of California, Los Angeles, has found that people who routinely kept daily gratitude journals showed more activity in the medial prefrontal cortex, an area of the brain key to decision-making and empathy.

## The relationship between gratitude and happiness

Grateful people tend to be happier. While, in general, happiness seems to be an effect of gratitude, in many situations, it is possible to develop happiness by cultivating gratitude.

## Why Gratitude Makes Us Happy

Gratitude shifts the focus from what you don't have to what you do.

At the same time, it reduces covet jealousy and frustration- all of which hinder joy.

Relationships Experts say that communication is key to having a healthy relationship, and expressing gratitude is an important part of that. Saying thank you to others makes them feel appreciated and valued, and we are immersed in it, which decreases the likelihood of having negative feelings in a relationship. Maintaining strong relationships with others is important to staying healthy.

Possibly more powerful against bumps:

Grateful individuals often tend to be far better at recouping from bumpy rides. Thankfulness can assist one with a sight injury or less-than-optimal life occasions as a chance for development instead of victimization

Research: The University of Pennsylvania research found that a group of people writing and personally delivering a letter of gratitude to someone who had positively affected them immediately experiences a massive increase in happiness scores. This impact was greater than that from any other intervention, with benefits lasting for a month.

## The Effect of Gratitude on Physical Health

Gratitude has long been the darling of the wellness world, with countless studies proving its mental health benefits. But practicing gratitude isn't just beneficial for the mind. Gratitude is also associated with physical benefits that can help you live longer.

By maintaining your bodily muscles and increasing good healthy habits, gratitude helps promote physical health by reducing stress and anxiety.

## Health Benefits of Gratitude

Lowered Blood Pressure and Heart Disease: Studies show those who practice regular gratitude often have lower blood pressure and are at a lower risk of heart disease.

Improved sleep quality: People who kept a gratitude journal reported sleeping better before falling asleep. Practicing gratitude helps improve sleep because it reduces intrusive, unwanted thinking.

Better Immunity: Long-term stress weakens the immune system, and gratitude can reduce its effects by lowering cortisol and increasing the immune response.

Reduced Chronic Pain: People with chronic pain who consciously count their blessings report feeling less pain and being more able to manage their lives.

One study published in the journal Psychosomatic Medicine found that heart patients who participated in gratitude exercises had less inflammation and better heart rate variability than those who did not.

## Conclusion: Gratitude Holds the Power of Transformation

Research on gratitude demonstrates that it is more than experiencing a fleeting positive emotion. Gratitude is a basic mindset that retrains your brain for happiness and well-being.

# Chapter 12

# Why People Struggle with Gratitude

## It's Not Always Easy To Be Grateful

Gratitude is a powerful practice, but it doesn't always come naturally. Despite its proven benefits, many people find it difficult to feel or express gratitude, especially in challenging times. This chapter explores the common obstacles to gratitude, such as negativity bias, materialism, and entitlement. By understanding these barriers, we can develop strategies to overcome them and foster a more grateful mindset.

## The Negativity Bias of the Human Mind

Our brains have evolved to give more attention to negative experiences in order to survive potential threats, which can make it harder to enjoy the moment. If you stub your toe and then smile at the wagging tail of a passing dog, which experience are you more likely to reflect on later that night? The question might help to highlight a survival function in the way we process or make sense of our experiences. Hidden in the detail of this question is a clue to a fundamental aspect of how we relate to life itself. Neuropsychologists tell us that, as complex organisms, we have developed to perceive negative experiences more quickly and do so more urgently than we'd give to positive experiences. It's a trait that's been labeled the negativity bias. '

## How the Negativity Bias Affects Gratitude:

### An Overemphasis on Problems

The mind is more apt to seize upon what's missing, what's wrong, rather than what's right, so any uptick of joy or success will get buried.

### Trouble Detecting Minor Positives:

Simple everyday things such as a stranger's generosity, a sunny day, or the color of the leaves often go unnoticed. The human brain constantly compares expectations with reality and weighs what disappoints or poses a threat more heavily than what it can admire.

### Meditating on Misfortune:

Negative experiences are remembered longer than positive experiences, so it can be hard to refocus on gratitude.

For example, a person might accept multiple compliments from colleagues but focus on the sole piece of negative feedback, overshadowing the positive content of the feedback.

How to Get Over It:

Keep a gratitude journal: Listing three good things every day helps the brain store more positive mental space.

Mindfulness Exercises:

Keeping your thoughts in the present can stop rumination and cut down on overthinking. By clearing your mind of stressful thoughts, it's easier to enjoy the good moments as they come.

Materialism and the Hedonic Treadmill.

In a consumerist culture, materialism encourages an unending sense of dissatisfaction, making cultivating gratitude more difficult. The "hedonic treadmill" describes our tendency to continuously seek happiness from external achievements or acquisitions without an ultimate permanent increase in our level of happiness

## How Materialism Hurts Our Gratitude:

Comparison culture:

Comparison breeds envy, not gratitude, because one constantly measures oneself against what others have achieved or given.

Diminishing Returns,

The thrill of attaining something new dissipated quickly, creating a void that you needed to fill by acquiring more things.

Attachment to outcomes:

When we tether our inner peace to future external goals, it can be easy to overlook the meaning that's already sitting in front of us.

Example: Someone buys themself a new car, which makes them happy for some time, but they realise after some weeks that their friend has a better car, which downgrades the new car's value, thus decreasing their gratitude towards their own car.

How to Avoid It:

Shift Focus to Experiences:

Investing in meaningful experiences rather than material goods fosters lasting inner peace.

Being thankful for what you have now: Focus on what you have and how it improves your life rather than the next big thing.

How to Conquer Entitlement & Discontentment

A sense of entitlement—the feeling that you deserve certain privileges or outcomes—gets in the way of thankfulness by setting up high expectations that can't possibly be met. Oddly enough, when unrealistic expectations are not met, it leads to feelings of dissatisfaction, and dissatisfaction sabotages gratitude.

**Why Feeling Entitled Rots Your Appetite for Gratitude**:

<u>Unrealistic Standards</u>:

Continuously expecting perfection or ideal outcomes allows little to be grateful for what comes in reality.

<u>Focusing on What's Missing</u>.

Entitlement focuses attention on unfulfilled wants rather than fulfilled ones, making chronic dissatisfaction inevitable.

## Failure to Acknowledge the Contributions of Others.

Taking people's goodwill or support for granted is corrosive to relationships and offers fewer opportunities to feel gratitude.

For instance, you might be angry with your team leader for not recognising your hard work and putting you forward for promotion while ignoring the fact that they have been incredibly supportive, mentored, coached, or given you great opportunities to grow.

### How to Overcome It

Adopt a Beginner's Mindset: Approach situations with curiosity and humility and enjoy small blessings.

Focus on contributions: Think about the people or circumstances that have aided your success rather than concentrating solely on your work.

Ways to Cultivate Gratitude

Reframe Problems:

Instead of seeing obstacles as barriers, view them as opportunities to learn and grow.

"I appreciate that this challenging project will help me grow new skills."

**Practice "Gratitude for the Small Stuff"** :

Develop a sense of gratitude for little things, such as a fresh cup of coffee, a stranger's smile, or a quiet walk.

Limit Comparison:

Minimize time on social media or elsewhere that leads to envy and redirect that energy to your individual goals.

Practice Gratitude Exercises:

Practices like writing thank-you notes or making a gratitude jar can help make the practice feel more concrete.

### Conclusion: Gratitude as a Choice

While barriers to gratitude are real, they are not insurmountable. By understanding the psychological and societal forces that make gratitude challenging, we can take proactive steps to cultivate it in our lives. Gratitude is not just a feeling; it's a choice to focus on abundance rather than lack and on connection rather than isolation. The next chapter will explore practical ways to make gratitude a daily habit through simple yet powerful practices.

# Chapter 13: Daily Gratitude Practices

## Building a Habit of Gratitude

Gratitude is a muscle: the more you utilize it, the more powerful it gets. When you exercise gratitude consistently, you make certain the advantages of thankfulness become a consistent part of your life. This chapter covers ways to exercise gratefulness daily, consisting of journaling and meditation, as well as how to strengthen your relationships, improve your mental well-being, and feel content through gratitude

### Maintaining an appreciation journal.

Among the simplest and most effective ways to express gratitude is to keep a journal. Listing what you're thankful for will certainly help you shift your focus from what you lack to what you have.

**Developing an Attitude of Gratitude**.

How to Begin:

Pick a format:

Use a physical notebook, digital app, or Word document – whichever you think you'll find easiest to access.

Set a time

Spare a few minutes daily—perhaps during your morning coffee or right before bed—to consciously think about what you're grateful for.

Be specific.

Try to avoid writing vague things like “I’m grateful for my family” and be more specific about your day, she says. “I’m grateful for the way my sister called to check on me today.”

Why should you...

Include a brief note about why each one is important to you, as this deepens your emotional connection to the practice.

Example Entry: "Today, I’m grateful for the sunny weather because it lifted my mood and made my walk more enjoyable."

Benefits:

1. Boosts mood and emotional well-being.
2. It helps you focus on the positives in your day.
3. You can develop a meaningful moments log so that you can look back on it when the times get tough.

## The Power of 'Thank You' in Relationships

When you communicate your gratitude directly to the person, you build your relationship and form deeper connections. Expressing gratitude with a simple "thank you" may sometimes feel like a common courtesy. But saying "thank you" to others is much more than that—it's a relationship-building tool that makes the recipient feel appreciated and valued by you and helps you experience genuine gratitude.

**How to Incorporate 'Thank You' Into Everyday Life:**

Positive Verbal Feedback:

Get into the habit of thanking people! B it for their input in the meeting, their contribution to a group project, or for cooking dinner.

Written records:

Sending an email or writing a note to thank you is a thoughtful way of showing appreciation on more personal terms. A simple gesture goes a long way.

Public recognition:

Thank someone publicly. If appropriate to the situation, you may publicly thank someone, such as in a meeting or workplace, or by mentioning the person on social media. Public recognition will make the person feel appreciated and boost morale in the organization or group.

Be Specific.

Instead of just saying "thank you" in a general fashion, specify what you are thanking the person for. "Thank you for staying late to help me finish the project" is more memorable than a passively said "thanks."

Consider a parent who shows gratitude to their child for helping with chores by saying, “I really appreciate you taking the time to clean your room without being asked. It means a lot to me,”.

Human-generated benefits:

1. Builds more trust and intimacy in your relationship.
2. Encourages others to continue with positive behaviours.
3. Decreases conflict.

Gratitude Meditation Techniques

One of the best ways to reconnect to yourself and deepen your appreciation of the now is through gratitude meditation.

Gratitude meditation is a form of mindfulness meditation that focuses on expressing gratitude for the things in your life.

Steps to Practice Gratitude Meditation:

Find a quiet place.

Find a comfortable, quiet place where you can sit or lie down.

Take deep breaths

Begin by noticing your breathing. Breathe in through your nose and slowly out through your mouth.

Practice gratitude.

Recall three things you're thankful for. These can be people, experiences, or even simple things like the sun on your face or a nice meal.

Imagine and feel:

When you think of each one, picture it in your mind's eye and focus on the good feelings it brings you. Feel grateful.

Conclude with affirmations.

Conclude your meditative exercise with affirmations: "I am surrounded by abundance" or "I am grateful for the blessings in my life."

Tip: Start with five to ten-minute sessions and gradually increase the length of your practice as you become more familiar or comfortable with the practice.

**Pros:**

1. It can reduce stress and anxiety.
2. Enhances positive emotionality.
3. Fosters a sense of serenity and satisfaction.

## Marrying Practices for Maximum Impact

While these gratitude practices can stand alone, integrating them can create a more well-rounded gratitude practice. For example:

Try starting your day by doing a gratitude meditation.

Keep a gratitude journal at night to refocus on the good during the day.

Each day, thank someone verbally or write a thank you note to someone.

The key to nurturing gratitude is consistency and repetition. Together, these practices help you build sustainable rhythms for nourishing gratitude and helping it blossom in all areas of your life.

## Conclusion: The Ripple Effect of Daily Gratitude

By making gratitude a routine part of your life, you can contribute to your well-being and the well-being of the people around you. Through three key gratitude practices of journaling, verbalizing gratitude to others, and meditation, you can enjoy more satisfying relationships, more emotional resilience, and a greater sense of joy and fulfillment. In the next chapter, I'll discuss how gratitude can also be a healing force in your life, especially when it comes to trauma and emotional pain.

# Chapter:14

# Gratitude as a Pathway to Healing

## The Role of Gratitude in Healing Trauma

Trauma leaves deep scars, often making it difficult to see beyond pain and loss. Yet, research and personal experiences suggest that gratitude can be a powerful tool for healing. Gratitude doesn't erase trauma, but it can shift perspectives, promote emotional resilience, and create a sense of meaning even in the face of profound challenges. This chapter explores the science behind gratitude and trauma recovery, how it shifts perspectives on past pain, and its use as a spiritual and emotional healing tool.

## Research around Gratitude and PTSD Recovery

Those living with post-traumatic stress disorder (PTSD) often spend a lot of time stuck in cycles of fear, anger, and sadness. Though traditional treatment methods remain a priority, gratitude practices have also been proven to effectively supplement these with positive emotions, helping to reduce stress.

**Key Findings**:

Decreased PTSD Symptoms:

Gratitude-practicing individuals have been found in studies to experience fewer PTSD symptoms, such as intrusive thoughts and emotional numbing. Gratitude helps shift attention away from agonizing recollections to positive elements in life.

## Enhanced Emotional Stability:

Gratitude turns on our brain's reward system. When feeling gratitude, our brain releases dopamine and serotonin (both of which are often low in people with PTSD/trauma), which helps to create a sense of safety and emotional peace and happiness.

## Improved sleep quality:

Trauma survivors have benefited from gratitude practices such as journaling to unlock happiness or calm excessive stress responses, frequently marked by insomnia or nightmares. People who are grateful feel less pain, stress, and insomnia and experience healthier relationships with improved mental and physical health.

Case Study: A veteran suffering from PTSD began a gratitude journal as part of his recovery. As he learned to focus on the small positives in his life (supportive friendships, etc.), he began to have fewer flashbacks and felt as if he had more control over his emotions.

### How gratitude shifts perspectives on past pain

One of the hardest parts of trauma can be making peace with the past. Gratitude doesn't negate the pain; it is redecorating it through new eyes, allowing survivors to find growth and meaning in it.

## Perspective-Shifting Benefits

Finding the good in a bad situation:

Gratitude can assist in identifying moments of support, perseverance, or personal growth within the context of a traumatic narrative. For instance, acknowledging the strength required to endure or the generosity of those who provided assistance.

How to Stop Ruminating:

Traumatic experiences can cause the mind to replay negative thoughts. Gratitude interrupts this process by allowing us to pause, notice, and reflect on the positive aspects of our lives, even if they appear small, and creates a buffer against the stress and anxiety from trauma.

Fostering post-traumatic growth.

Post-traumatic growth is the positive change that happens after you struggle with something really hard. Gratitude supports post-traumatic growth by helping you see the lessons you learned, the closeness you enhanced, or the purpose you discovered.

Example: A woman who lost her home in a natural disaster used gratitude to focus on the kindness of strangers who offered shelter and support, helping her rebuild her life and her hope.

## The Place of Gratitude in Spiritual and Holistic Practices for Wellbeing

When you experience trauma, your identity, purpose, and relationship to yourself, others, and the world are also traumatized. Gratitude is a way to revitalize those things by helping to restore a sense of spiritual connection and purpose and feeling connected to other people.

**Spiritual benefits of gratitude**?

Connecting to Something Bigger:

Gratitude tends to propel individuals into a state of wonder and awe, whether it's rooted in feeling engulfed by the beauty of nature, the glory of God, or the goodness of humankind. That can offer solace and meaning in the aftermath of trauma.

Faith in Humanity:

Saying "thank you" when people do things for us restores our faith in humanity and helps disrupt the cycle that trauma creates, making us feel isolated and distrustful of other people.

Galloping Grief:

Gratitude drives people to be attentive to what they've gained, even after a loss. Often, that generates a sense of purpose and inspires them to give back.

For example, people who have survived trauma often report feeling a newfound gratitude for the simple joys of life, such as a good cup of coffee, the chance to see a sunrise, someone's smile, or a moment of peace. In this way, these simple pleasures help them to slowly reassemble a sense of being connected to this world.

## Actionable Gratitude Practices for Trauma Healing

1. Gratitude Journaling:

Write about one thing each day that provided a feeling of peace, joy, or connection. Think small, i.e., a nice conversation with someone or a comforting meal.

2. Gratitude Notes:

Write a letter to someone who supported you during a difficult time. Whether or not you send it, the act of writing fosters reflection on positive connections.

3. Nature-Based Gratitude

Spend some time outside soaking in the nature that surrounds you. Pay attention to the beauty all around you, and think about how nature itself gives us a sense of renewal and even-keel.

4. Gratitude Meditation Gruppen:

Meditations that focus on healing and gratitude can be helpful, as they help one visualize or contemplate moments in which one was supported or comforted.

## Conclusion: Gratitude as a Companion in Healing

Healing from trauma is a complex and deeply personal journey. Gratitude doesn't erase the pain but provides a path toward resilience, perspective, and peace. Focusing on what is good amidst the challenges can rebuild your sense of connection, purpose, and emotional balance. The next chapter will explore how gratitude can transform not only individuals but also workplaces, communities, and society at large.

# Chapter 15:

# The Gratitude Chapter: Leadership and the Common Good

## Gratitude Beyond the Self

Although gratitude is often seen as an individual practice, its benefits are significant, collective, and transformative. In leadership, workplaces, and community settings, gratitude fosters and sustains the structural and organizational systems of collaboration as well as strong relationships based on trust, commitment, and hard work. This chapter explores how gratitude-based habits can reshape organizational cultures, empower social movements, and instill gratitude values in younger generations through education and practice.

## How Gratitude Can Transform Your Workplace

Workplaces succeed when workers feel valued and grateful. Gratitude is essential for leadership and teamwork, not a "nice-to-have."

The Benefits of Gratitude on the Job:

Boosted Employee Engagement:

Appreciated employees feel more motivated and engaged in their jobs. Gratitude from leaders can lead to increased morale and job satisfaction.

S

tronger Team Chemistry:

Gratitude creates a culture of collaboration as it inspires team members to appreciate each other's efforts.

Decreased Stress:

Gratitude reduces stress in the workplace by cultivating an environment where workers feel more supported and valued.

For example, a manager who consistently expresses gratitude towards their team for their hard work, privately and publicly, will likely create a positive feedback cycle that increases proactivity and trust.

**How leaders can inspire gratitude**.

Personal recognition:

Show employees you appreciate them for their unique contributions, regardless of their department. Avoid giving generalized praise.

Recognition Programs:

Introduce programs celebrating efforts, like Employee of the Month or peer-nominated awards.

Meetings of Gratitude:

Devote the start of your team meetings to gratitude, giving each participant a chance to give a “shout out” to another person (or project) they're thankful for.

Insight: Teams with leaders who express gratitude perform 50% better on collaborative tasks than teams who don’t, according to a study in Harvard Business Review.

## Social Movements Based on Thanks and Giving Back

Gratitude has the potential to bring people together and galvanise action. Indeed, social movements grounded in appreciation and giving back have prompted positive change throughout history.

Illustrations of Gratitude in Action:

Pay It Forward:

Initiatives like the "Pay It Forward" movement encourage individuals to act kindly to generate momentum of goodwill and gratitude.

Gratitude-Focused Charities:

Organizations such as Charity: Water and Feeding America are examples of how giving can be a way of showing gratitude for the abundance so many of us share.

Song of the Common Man: From the Bottom Up!

Community gardens, volunteer organizations, and neighborhood groups often build up around a sense of shared gratitude and responsibility.

Case Study: Communities often demonstrate thanks to first responders and volunteer workers by banding together and instilling the expression of gratitude in their community in the wake of natural disasters.

**How to Cultivate Gratitude at a Societal Level**:

Volunteer Opportunities - Encourage involvement in local or global initiatives to cultivate gratitude and spread kindness.

Gratitude Days: Advocate for events like "World Gratitude Day" to raise awareness and celebrate acts of appreciation.

**How to Teach Children Gratitude**

Teaching our children to be grateful is one of the most powerful things we can do to cultivate a culture of appreciation for generations to come. Gratitude helps kids make friends, boosts athletic performance, and encourages them to give back to their communities.

**How do you teach gratitude**?

<u>Be thankful.</u>

Kids learn by example. Thank your server. Thank your child's teacher. Thank your partner. Do it in front of your kids.

<u>Gratitude Ritual:</u>

Create family rituals centered on gratitude, such as naming one thing you're thankful for at dinner or before bed.

Interactive Activities:

Get children involved with gratitude practices, like building a "gratitude tree" or sending thank-you notes to teachers and friends.

Volunteer together:

Take kids to volunteer to help others – whether working in a food bank or cleaning up litter in a local park. Taking kids to serve others helps them appreciate what they have and develops empathy from a very young age.

Example: A school introduced a "Gratitude Journal" initiative, encouraging students to write daily entries on what they were grateful for. Teachers observed enhanced classroom behavior and a more positive climate.

## Conclusion: Building a Thanks-Based Culture

Gratitude can transform us as individuals and build transformative communities, organisations, and movements. With leadership, social movements, and education that nurture appreciation, we can cultivate a culture of connection, kindness, and giving back. In this final chapter, we'll explore the exercises that can deepen your gratitude practice and how to bring such practice to bear on all aspects of life.

# Chapter 16: Practical Exercises on Gratitude

## Turning gratitude into action

Gratitude has its greatest impact when it moves from being a feeling to being a practice. Whether you have never thought of being grateful before or it's second nature to you, having actionable ways to practice gratitude will make it much more effective. The exercises in this chapter offer a range of ways to help you cultivate gratitude, build stronger relationships, and create longer-lasting feelings of happiness.

### 21-Day Gratitude Challenge

A 21-day challenge is a powerful tool for building a gratitude habit and seamlessly integrating it into your life. By dedicating yourself to small, daily acts, you can teach your mind to focus on the positive and abundance.

How it works:

Day 1-7 Gratitude Journaling:

Write down three things you're grateful for each day. Be specific and include why these things are important to you.

Days 8–14: Expressing thanks to others:

Every weekday, send a simple note, text, or verbal acknowledgment of thanks to someone in your life. The emphasis is less on format and more on authenticity and specificity.

Days 15-21: Reflective Thanks

Spend five to ten minutes daily picking a past difficulty or challenge that taught you something important and write about the way it helped you grow.

**Pros:**

1. Enhances regular practice of gratitude.
2. Building bonds with others and personal resilience.
3. Lays the groundwork for lasting good habits.

## Writing a Letter of Gratitude

A gratitude letter is a meaningful exercise in which you express appreciation to someone who has positively impacted your life. Whether you actually share the letter or not, simply writing it can be an equally transformational experience.

How to Write a Gratitude Letter:

Select the Recipient:

Do you know someone who makes a difference in your life—a mentor, a friend, a family member, or a colleague?

Be specific:

Explain what they did and the effect it had on you. Make it meaningful, as well as focus on the details to make gratitude truly heartfelt.

Express your emotions:

Share the type of impact they've had on you, including how it made you feel and how you've changed for the better because of it.

Deliver (Optional):

If you're open to the idea, hand-deliver the letter or mail it. Watching their reaction can have an even more emotional impact.

Example: A student writes to their high school teacher and thanks them for inspiring a love of learning and reassuring them during a difficult time.

**Benefits**:

Strengthening emotional connections.

Offers closure while deepening relationships.

It can enhance both your mood and the mood of the person receiving it.

Gratitude Jar Method

A gratitude jar is a fun way to have a tangible record of things you are appreciative of over the course of the year.

How to Make a Gratitude Jar:

Pick a Jar:

Use a clear jar or container so you can see your offspring growing over time.

Make Gratitude Slips:

Scatter small pieces of paper and a pen nearby to capture moments of gratitude as they happen.

Make it a daily or weekly habit:

Write down one thing you're grateful for each day or week and put it in the jar.

Year-End Review:

At the end of the year, go through the slips to read the magic and happy moments from the year.

Tip: Get members of the family or coworkers involved — and gain a collective perspective — by asking them to contribute to a communal gratitude jar.

Advantages:

Encourages mindfulness and daily reflection.

Offers a tangible reminder of life's blessings.

Creates a positive environment in families or teams.

**Gratitude Walks**

The combination of gratitude and exercise can supercharge their benefits because they engage the mind and body. Walking while contemplating what you're grateful for is known as gratitude walking.

How to Do It:

Find a Calm Environment:

Pick a quiet park, neighborhood, or nature trail.

Set an intention:

Before you start, decide that you will focus on gratitude during this walk. Perhaps you dedicate this walk to being grateful for your health, the environment, or a particular person.

Morning Walk Reflection:

With each step, think about something that you're grateful for. Either say what you're thinking silently in your head or speak softly out loud.

Notice Your Surroundings:

Notice the beauty of nature, such as the sounds of the birds, the trees blowing in the breeze, the sun shining brightly, and the calmness of the water on the beach.

**Benefits include**:

Underscores a blend of physical and emotional health.

Enhances mindfulness and attitude of total appreciation for living in the present moment.

Reducing stress and increasing relaxation.

**Gratitude Random Acts**

Unexpected expressions of gratitude bring delight and connection. The simple act of reaching out to someone just to say thank you can create a small moment of happiness and cultivate your sense of community.

**Creative Ways to Say Thank You**

Write a quick thank-you note and leave it for a coworker, barista, or neighbor.

Pay It Forward:

Pay for someone's coffee, toll, or meal as a random act of kindness.

Surprise Someone:

Bring a small gift, like flowers or a small gift, such as flowers or a favorite treat.

Volunteer your time:

Offer your talents or time to someone who could use it or to a local organization.

**Benefits:**

Fosters an attitude of gratitude.

Builds a sense of community.

Name something that snowballs into an avalanche in the best possible sense.

## Conclusion: Making Gratitude a Lifestyle

Gratitude is a lifelong journey that changes the way you experience the world and interact with people. It is more than a passing feeling. These are only a few ideas for how you can make your gratitude practice more effective.

# Chapter 17:

# What Is Love

## Love

It's just a small, four-letter word that lies at the root of our deepest joys, profound agonies, and most meaningful relationships. It has inspired artists of every kind, bonded families, and propelled our species forward. Yet, love is surprisingly difficult to define for something so central to the human experience. Is it an emotion? A choice? A biological response to external stimuli? The answer is that it's all those things—and so much more.

This chapter examines love, its different types, the science of how love works, and the deeper spiritual meaning of unconditional love. After reading it, your perception of love will change in ways you never imagined.

## The Many Faces of Love

Love makes the world go around, right? It can be hard and soft, wild and tamed. How can one word with so few letters describe something that can be the best — and worst — part of living? Psychologists, sociologists, anthropologists, philosophers, and poets have all come up with different categories of love. Here are some of the best known.

### Romantic love

Romantic love is the most common one. This is the one that comes to mind first.

The butterflies in our stomachs, throwing random glances at each other in the hallway, the racing of our hearts when we are together. It is addictive and exciting, passionate, filled with emotions, and at times, irrational. In the real love life cycle, romantic love only marks the beginning. It transforms and grows into companionate love as the partners get to know each other better. The possessiveness realized in the "honeymoon stage" gradually fades, and the heady feelings wane, giving place to something deeper and long-lasting – based on common interest and values, companionship, respect, mutual trust, and commitment.

But romantic love isn't always easy — it takes commitment, communication, and sometimes, forgiveness to make it last.

**Family love**

This is the love we feel for our family members: parents, siblings, children, and chosen family. Familial love is unconditional and is built upon mutual respect for each other. One feels a natural bond with family; familial love is a powerful bond. However, familial love isn't reliant on blood or family; oftentimes, there can be a deep friendship with family members, and love is a byproduct of this familiarity. Familial love is very different from all other types of love.

**Self-love**

People often misinterpret self-love. It isn't a haughty, selfish, self-centred sort of love. To love oneself is to acknowledge one's own potential and treat oneself like someone worthy of that potential. You can't function in a healthy relationship without self-love. This love entails understanding boundaries, practicing self-care, and turning off that annoying inner voice that tells you that you aren't good enough. Consider this the type of love upon which all other love can rest.

**Universal Love**

The last type of love is selfless love and mankind. Universal love is love tied to altruism, kindness, and compassion. It is love that, rather than being tied to certain qualities in a person, is felt universally to everyone. Universal love connects us to our humanity and to something greater than ourselves. It is why we want to help others, fight for justice and equality, or conserve the planet. Universal love takes us beyond ourselves and gives us a sense of belonging to the greater cosmos. Universal love is a shared love and a reminder that we are all more alike than we are different.

Although love may seem to be too magical to understand, there is a science to it. When you fall in love, a few chemicals are released in the brain, which causes the emotional feelings of love in your body.

It starts with oxytocin. Sometimes called the "love hormone," oxytocin is released with bonding activities — like hugging, kissing, or looking into someone's eyes. It's the hormone that bonds mothers to their babies. It's the hormone that causes us to feel safe in relationships and close to the people we love most.

But neuromodulators like oxytocin aren't the only brain chemicals involved in romance. The "feel-good" neurotransmitter dopamine rushes to your brain in the early stages of romantic love, generating excitement and euphoria. If you've ever felt high on love, you can thank dopamine for that. But as relationships progress, serotonin levels increase, resulting in feelings of calm and peace.

Although love may be biological—therefore primal and seemingly less magical—this does not diminish its significance. In fact, one could argue that love is essential for our species' survival and is deeply ingrained in our emotional well-being on an individual level. It indicates that our brains are hardwired to seek love.

**Unconditional Love**: The Highest Form Unconditional love is viewed as the highest form of love. It is selfless, characterized by absolute trust, and given without asking for anything in return. Unconditional love is not based on any conditions; it is infinite and not based on expectations. For example, unconditional love can be the love a parent has for their child. This love can be found in a romantic relationship, a friendship, or even towards a derek person.

## Spiritual unconditional love

" is very similar because it means loving people simply for who they are, warts and all," Parmar said. Spiritually, unconditional love signifies loving all living beings. Unconditional love is practiced across many spiritual traditions and religions. In Christianity, it's referred to as agape; in Buddhism, it's known as metta, or loving-kindness. Spiritual unconditional love encompasses the same acceptance as it does in romantic and platonic relationships, but agape and metta call for something a bit deeper on a spiritual level. They emphasize the importance of demonstrating these forms of love to all living beings.

Practicing unconditional love doesn't always mean it is easy. There will be moments that aren't fun, and you'll need to practice patience, forgiveness, and letting go of judgments, but when you can, you can unlock the greatest sense of peace and fulfillment.

### Why Love Matters: How Affection Shapes Lives

Love isn't just a "nice to have." It's a fundamental part of what makes us human. Studies have shown that people who experience strong, loving relationships—whether romantic, familial, or platonic—tend to live longer, healthier, and happier lives. Love reduces stress, strengthens our immune systems, and even helps us recover from illness faster.

Beyond its personal health benefits, love gives us something or someone to live for. It motivates us to write poems and songs and imagine gods and afterlives. It spurs us to join others, even in the smallest ways, to make the world more beautiful and often more just. Love is the thing that makes life sing; it provides the melody and motivation for so much we do to make our lives worthwhile.

**Love is complex and unpredictable**.

At one moment, it fills your heart to the brim, and the next, it leaves you shattered. It's as complex as it is beautiful. As an essential part of life, love connects us all. This universal bond holds families together, unifies strangers, and inspires us to explore uncharted territories. Whether you're experiencing your first love, forming a new connection, or seeking to fall in love again, one thing remains constant—love is life's greatest experience.

# Chapter 18:

# The Psychology Of Self-love

**Self-love.**

We hear it all the time—I've said it countless times myself (whether in conversations with loved ones or in other articles I've written) because it's so important. But what exactly does self-love mean? Does it mean taking bubble baths and deep conditioning your hair? Does it mean face masks? Or is it something much deeper and an essential skill we must practice in order to obtain inner peace? Or all of the above?

In this chapter, we'll examine the psychology of self-love, its effects on mental health, and how we can overcome the obstacles that prevent us from loving ourselves completely. Most importantly, we'll explore how self-love is different from narcissism and why accepting it is one of the most powerful things you can do for yourself.

Why Loving Yourself Affects You

Your Mental Health Self-love is really about acceptance and care. It's being able to look inwards, flaws, imperfections, and all and see someone worthwhile of love and respect. Why is that important for mental health?

Building resilience

Loving yourself allows you to bounce back better when life throws you curve balls. Self-love gives you the stability and grounding necessary to withstand inevitable life challenges, including relationship or work-related hardships. "When you're able to apply the concept of self-love to challenging life events, you'll be better able to bounce back and weather those storms, which builds resilience, confidence, and self-worth. As a result, you're less likely to rely on resilience from another person and get down on yourself if your relationship ends," says Nesheiwat. Self-love helps you work to move on after failure. "This helps them more easily move on and accept their mistakes and persevere, as they are less likely to take the failure personally and have a better understanding that failing and learning is a part of life," says Nesheiwat.

Lowering Stress and Anxiety

Self-love helps to lower stress and anxiety, too. When you're nice to yourself, you don't get caught up in negativity or torture yourself over mistakes. You cultivate a mind state that prioritizes growth rather than self-assassination. This lowers cortisol levels and makes you feel more relaxed.

Build Strong And Healthy Relationships.

Your takeaway? You cannot pour from an empty cup. If you don't have love and acceptance for yourself, you cannot build healthy, meaningful relationships. The way you feel about yourself puts a quality out in the world about how you should be treated; if you hold yourself high, you will attract other people who hold you high.

## Getting Rid Of Self-Criticism along with Self-Doubt

For a lot of us, self-love does not come naturally. We're growing up in a world that conditions us to believe that we're only worthy if we achieve certain things, look certain ways, or have certain statuses. We're growing up with internal critics who can't stand us and tell us daily that we aren't good enough.

How do you silence your inner critic, the nagging voice in your head that tells you not to go after things you want and shut the door on self-doubt?

Challenge Negative Thoughts

When your inner critic starts its monologue, pause and ask yourself: "Is this thought helpful? Is it even true?"

Often, the harsh things we tell ourselves are based on fear or insecurity, not reality. Practice replacing these thoughts with affirmations or kinder, more constructive messages.

Celebrate your success.

We're quick to judge ourselves harshly when things go awry — but when was the last time you gave yourself props when things go right? Spend more time basking in the glory of your wins, no matter how small. Did you survive a difficult day? Follow through on a commitment to a friend? Those are wins worthy of celebrating.

## Practice Self-Compassion

Self-compassion is the antidote to self-criticism. Instead of judging yourself harshly, try speaking to yourself the way you would a close friend. When you make a mistake, remind yourself that you're human—and humans are imperfect.

## Self-Love versus Narcissism

A prevailing myth around self-love is that it's selfish or narcissistic. But nothing could be further from the truth.

### Narcissism and self-love

Self-love is grounded in self-acceptance. Self-love means recognising that you aren't perfect while loving the whole of yourself. It's rooted in humility and an acknowledgement that your worth doesn't depend on external markers.

Narcissism Needs External Validation
Narcissism, on the other hand, is often a disguise for insecurity. It's a behavioral pattern that involves a need for constant praise, an inflated sense of self-importance, and a lack of empathy for others. While self-love is rooted in creating a sense of internal confidence, narcissism relies on the need for external validation to feel worthy.

In a nutshell, self-love gives you more connection with yourself, while narcissism robs you even of the deepest and closest connection possible in life: the one with yourself.

Steps to Cultivate Self-love

If self-love feels challenging, it's possible to practice it. Over time, these steps will become more natural. If you notice that making time and space for yourself is really difficult, you can look to a trained mental health professional for compassion and guidance. What do you see when you look in the mirror? Notice how you feel when you take the time to look at yourself. Are you critical? Do you see something you like? Or do you avoid looking at your reflection altogether? No matter what you see, take a moment to speak out loud with compassion to yourself.

Try saying: I love you. You are beautiful. You're enough. Or you can say something unique to you. The small practice of tuning into how you relate to your reflection is small but mighty.

For example, you can make lovingly caring for your body part of your daily routine. Massage oil into your skin, dance naked in front of your mirror, or cultivate tons of pleasure in a self-love, self-pleasure practice. A big part of developing self-love is tuning inward and reaching for self-discovery. This allows you to fully understand what is happening with your emotions, experience, and perspective.

Keeping a journal of your experience means that you can put pen to paper and let your mind and heart explore what is happening inside, without pressure or judgment. Think of self-love mantras like maintenance work for your mind. As you extend new thoughts, ideas, and attitudes toward yourself, you build new grooves in your brain. It becomes a natural, deeply ingrained part of who you are with time.

Finding balance in social life is a big part of self-care and self-love. While strong, supportive relationships are an important part of caring for yourself, you do need to find the balance of how social environments, activities, and people serve you.

For example, if you tend to say “yes” a lot—constantly making plans or finding yourself in stressful relationships or don’t offer support- try developing healthy boundaries by spending less time tending to others. Or, if you tend to isolate or feel uncomfortable around people, reach out to like-minded people or spend time out in environments like parks or coffee shops where you can be around social activity. Sure, self-care is spoken of a lot as bubble baths and doing your hair or nails, but it can be as simple as getting yourself a cup of water. Often, “catching up” on self-care tasks can feel overwhelming or time-consuming while you’re busy, so try adopting small practices into your daily routine. You can even start with 15 minutes a day and build from there!

For example, get that nourishing meal that you’ve been meaning to cook for yourself started. Sit down and call the doctor for that nagging injury that’s been bothering you. Open a single window and feel the fresh air in your space. Make a playlist of songs you love and play it while you pack lunch. Cooking is an act of self-love. It allows you to tune into the full experience through all five of your senses. Cooking yourself a nourishing meal—a simple or complex meal that tunes into your needs and celebrates your self-worth through the act of care and nourishment. Bonus points if you source ingredients from farmers or local harvests!

We all need reminders of the unique greatness we all habit. Try to celebrate yourself in some way. Spend money on yourself to do or buy something that feels really good. Or simply plot out some time in the near future that you can dedicate to celebrating or pampering yourself. Celebrate or pamper yourself with friends or by yourself in an act of love and luxury. Hold yourself in your heart. Try placing your hands on your heart or wrapping them around your shoulders. Ask yourself how you're doing or what you need—and gently listen for an answer.

Many practices that people turn to are taken from experiences of differing cultures. Try delving deep into the practices of your own heritage and lineage. Cultivate recipes, practices, and cultural values into your daily practices. Creating a small ritual and space for yourself allows you to hold space for who you are and what you need. Plan out how you'd like your sacred space to look and feel. What could you include to reflect yourself? Think about what you need from a meditation practice and how you'd like to ask for it. Adjust recipes and practices, and dance lovingly toward your inner being.

Start a gratitude practice for your mind, body, and soul. Practicing self-love can be as simple as getting a glass of water. Self-compassion and acts of grace for yourself will be a practice that evolves over time. Tune inward and listen for what feels authentic and aligned to you—knowing self-love, time, practice, and guidance will allow it to become a more natural part of your life.

### Establish Boundaries

Saying no isn't selfish; it's necessary. Setting boundaries is one way to protect your energy and ensure you aren't overextending yourself to accommodate others. Remember, you're entitled to your well-being.

### Make Self-Care a Priority

Self-care isn't just about pampering yourself (though that can be part of it!). It's about meeting your physical, emotional, and mental needs. That might mean getting enough sleep, eating nutritious food, or taking time to pursue a hobby you love.

Surround Yourself with Supportive People

The people you hang out with can influence the way you view yourself. Be around people who love you, encourage you, and support you. Choose friends and family who remind you of your worth.

Make Use of Manifestation

There is no perfect, and chasing perfect will rob you of the good. Seek progress, not perfection. Be satisfied with your good efforts, lawful results, and all.

**Why Self-Love Matters**

Perfection is unrealistic, but self-love, on the other hand, is attainable. For most of us, self-love is treating yourself with the same kindness, respect, and compassion as you would treat a friend, family member, or partner. "It's not about attaining anything; it's about believing you're enough," says Amber Wright, MA, LMFT. "If you are striving for goals and perfection, then you focus on the striving. When you focus on self-love, then you focus on yourself."

When you love yourself, life becomes a little easier: You tackle challenges with confidence, you form healthier relationships, and ultimately, you find a sense of calm that isn't so easily shaken up by the stormy periods that inevitably come around. Self-love isn't a luxury; it's a necessity.

Loving yourself is truly one of the greatest things you can do for yourself and the world. As you step into the light of your self-love, you give others permission to do the same. You model what it means to shine brightly in this world. You model what it means to be unapologetically you. In whatever ways those words resonate with you, you model what it means to live a life of truth, beauty, and abundance. You create a ripple effect of kindness and acceptance that carries far greater weight than you'll ever know. So go ahead, take that first step. You're worth it.

# Chapter 19:

# Love in Relationships

Love may be recognized as the essential ingredient at the heart of all relationships. But what does it take to cultivate it, let alone maintain it truly? Relationships—whether romantic, familial, or platonic—are often where people discover the deepest love and where that love faces its greatest challenges. From apologies, forgiveness, and gratitude to understanding love languages, this chapter will delve into how love deepens and becomes more sophisticated, influencing our relationships.

## How to Tell if You're in a Healthy Relationship

Mutual respect:

Each person values who the other is and understands the other person's boundaries.

Open Communication:

Constructive, open, honest, and respectful dialogue is encouraged and expected, even for the most difficult conversations.

Support and Encouragement:

You encourage one another's growth. Each partner is supportive of the others.

Balanced and independent:

You stay true to your own self but are deeply connected.

## Signs of Toxic Love

Control and manipulation:

One partner might use his/her influence to persuade the other to do something or use guilt to get a desire or goal.

Trust Issues:

Jealousy and suspicion erode the trust needed for a relationship to function properly.

Codependent Partnerships:

Individuals in codependent partnerships lean too heavily on one another to be emotionally stable. This can hinder personal growth and self-sufficiency.

Emotional neglect:

Having your needs and feelings ignored or dismissed.

Recognizing these dynamics is the first step toward change. If you're in a toxic relationship, seeking help—whether from a trusted friend, therapist, or support group—can help you navigate the path forward.

### Love Languages and How They Shape Connections

Have you ever felt like you were giving your all in a relationship, but the other person didn't seem to notice? This disconnect often comes down to love languages—how we give and receive love. Understanding love languages can transform relationships by helping us communicate affection in ways that truly resonate

**The 5 Love Languages by Dr. Gary Chapman lists five ways people show love.**

Words of Affirmation :

For people who prefer this love language, words (spoken and written) make all the difference. Hearing "I love you" or random compliments makes them feel more connected to their partner.

Acts of Service :

For these people, actions speak louder than words. Whether it's cooking a meal, running an errand, or helping with a project, these people appreciate when others do things to ease the responsibilities that they are shouldering.

Receiving Gifts

It's more about the thought and the meaning. A meaningful gift, no matter how small or inexpensive, can make someone feel loved and considered.

Quality Time

If your love language is quality time, you want your partner's undivided attention. Simply being in the same room as someone else doesn’t cut it; those who love quality time want to connect with others. They relish meaningful conversations and connections without outside noises or interruptions.

Touch

Hugs, kisses, and a stroked shoulder can all indicate affection for someone, with physical touch as their love language. People with this love language feel grounded in and appreciated through their physicality.

Understanding you and your loved ones/nannies and friends

Love languages can fill in the cracks and lead to closer, more meaningful relationships.

**Love as a Ground for Growth**:

A love that is nurtured and supported serves as a foundation for your growth. Love that provides security is the ground that allows you to face life's challenges bravely, knowing you have a person you can count on. That can encourage you to take risks, experiment, and become the best version of yourself.

Love-based relationships Aren't Perfect, But Rather Survivors. They're willing to weather the storms, endure the shifts, experience those shifts together, and emerge on the other side—better, stronger, and more durable than before. Love is a process, not a moment or a destination. Any time spent working on love is time well spent.

**Conclusion**: Love in Relationships Love is at the heart of every meaningful relationship. However, love alone cannot sustain a relationship. We heal and nurture our cherished connections through apology, forgiveness, and gratitude. We safeguard our hearts and mental well-being by recognizing the difference between healthy and toxic relationships. By understanding the various love languages, we foster bonds that are not only strong but can last a lifetime.

Relationships are where love actually happens. They allow us to experience all the joy, connection, and growth that comes from loving people. But more than that, they remind us of the most important truth about love: it's not something we have; it's something we do.

# Chapter 20:

# Love and Compassion for Strangers

Love and compassion should never be exclusive to those we know. Some of the most important, world-altering acts of love are toward strangers—people we might never meet again if we interact at all but for whom our acts of mercy and grace are crucially and irrevocably meaningful. We will discuss the power of altruism, the complexities of the psychology behind it, and why intervening when we can is so vital. We will also examine how acts of love can change entire lives and communities.

## Altruism and its Psychological Rewards

**Altruism** –

The unselfish concern for other people is the purest form of love. It motivates us to do things for others with no expectation of a reward to ourselves. It makes us hold the door open for the person behind us, pay compliments to others, and offer our seats to a stranger on a crowded tram. But why do humans do this? What is it about altruistic acts that drive us to help other people without getting anything obvious in return? How can being altruistic impact our mental health and happiness?

The Biology of Altruism :

Scientists have found that altruism is hardwired in the brain. That's right! Helping others triggers the brain to release feel-good chemicals, including oxytocin (the love hormone) and dopamine (the reward neurotransmitter), to create the "helper's high," much like the rush of endorphins that long-distance runners achieve. No wonder giving feels just as good—if not better—than receiving!

Emotional gains:

It's good for your mental health. Being nice to others doesn't just feel good — studies show it also has lasting health benefits. People who engage in random acts of kindness on a regular basis have lower levels of stress, decreased symptoms of depression, and overall a greater sense of life satisfaction.

Making friends with others:

Acts of selfless kindness possess a unique ability to bring people together — even if just for a moment — who might otherwise remain strangers. "We are all connected by our shared humanity, and we remember that when we take the time to do something for someone else," they say. "Cultivating this sense of connection, or belonging, can be very meaningful and powerful for both the helper and the person receiving help."

## Kindness That Counts

Sometimes, kindness crosses our paths by chance. Other times, it arrives intentionally, delivered by friends or strangers at precisely the moment we need it most. Kindness can be difficult to define because it's often the smallest, most unexpected gestures that make the biggest impact. It's the smile you didn't know you needed, the perfect gesture right when you need it, or the surprise gift of something special. Here is a collection of everyday moments of kindness, love, and compassion for strangers

Listening with Empathy

In a world of distractions, one of the simplest ways to love another person is to offer them the gift of listening. Whether it is a colleague processing a bad day at the office or a stranger sharing vulnerably, your willingness to attend is an important way to communicate that they are truly seen.

Paying it forward

Seemingly small, random acts of kindness—like paying for the coffee of the person behind you in line or leaving a note of encouragement for a co-worker—can have a significant impact. These gestures remind people that goodness exists in the world and increase the likelihood that they will pass on kindness to others.

One of the easiest ways to show compassion is to do something helpful for another person without expecting a reward in return. This could be as complex as going and volunteering at a local homeless shelter, or doing some charitable work to help raise donations for disaster relief funds, or something as simple as just giving someone a ride who has had their car break down, or has some other reason why they can't make it to a particular destination on their own, without assistance. Not only will this earn you the gratitude and admiration of friends, family members, colleagues, and other random strangers, it will also benefit you on an emotional and psychological level, because helping others helps us to feel good about ourselves, and gives us that "warm glow" that comes from knowing that we have given hope to those who needed it most!

## Speaking Out for Others

Love and compassion aren't always expressed in silence. Sometimes, love means speaking up on behalf of the marginalized, advocating for justice, or living in solidarity with those who are suffering. These acts of loving others illustrate that although love may be quiet, it's not passive.

## The Ripple Effect of Love in Communities

One of the most beautiful aspects of love is its ability to spread. When we show love and compassion to one person, it creates a ripple effect, inspiring others to do the same. This phenomenon has been observed in communities around the world.

## Contagious To Be Kind

Yes, studies have even found that kindness is contagious because seeing it makes us more likely to do it for someone else. Someone holds the door open for you, and you'll hold the door open for someone behind you. Our small acts of loving-kindness quickly add up and even encourage a culture of kindness.

Strengthening Communities.

When people come together and learn to love one another empathetically, amazing things can happen. Communities are strengthened, connections are created, and people are more willing to help each other rather than stand idly by. Whether a neighborhood joins together to hold a food drive or strangers rebuild after a natural disaster, these acts of collective love are strong testaments to the strength of unity.

Changing Lives

Sometimes, it only takes one small great act of love and compassion to change a person's life forever. We've all heard of a teacher who spent a little extra time with a student in need or a stranger who gave someone the words of encouragement they needed when they were going through a rough time, and both ended up changing the person's life forever. These simple but great acts of love and compassion remind us to stay gracious and give when we can because you never know who you might have an impact on, even years down the road.

## Reasons You Should Love People You Don't Know

At first glance, it appears we could survive by only loving those we're familiar with, those close to us. Why should we go out of our comfort zone to love complete, random strangers? Why love others, why love strangers, when it costs us energy, emotional investment, and vulnerability? The truth is that when we love others, we add to their lives and our own well-being.

Compassion towards strangers destroys all manner of stone walls—cultural, emotional, political, and ideological—and builds bridges in their place, inspiring and compelling communities to draw closer together. Through acts of love, we are reminded of our intrinsic similarity in light of our diversity.

**Conclusion: The World Needs Your Love.**

Acts of love and compassion for strangers might not win you any columns or medals, but they are some of the most important contributions we can make to the world.

Every kind word, generous act, and empathetic gesture makes the world a better place, inspiring a domino effect of kindness greater than anything you could imagine.

Here's the beauty of love: It doesn't need to be grand to make a difference. Love can be simple: holding the door open for someone, smiling at a stranger, or giving someone your ears for a few moments. These small moments remind us of the best parts of being human—and they can change the world, one small act of kindness at a time.

# Chapter 21:

# Love beyond death and time

Love surpasses our earthly bounds. It lives on in our hearts long after someone we love has left us, and it can connect us throughout time and space. In this chapter, we look at stories of love that illustrate how love can transcend time and life span. We also consider the soul connection theory, which proposes that love is forever.

Tales as Old as Time Love has long proven to defy time. There are many stories that remind us of the timeless nature of love.

Timeless Romances

Take the iconic story of Romeo and Juliet, which shows that love continued despite tragic circumstances. While fiction, these stories contain an eternal truth: Love is eternal in nature and lives far beyond what life may throw in its path.

In real life, couples who are separated by war, illness, or distance, defying the odds, find their way back to each other. Love seems to have a funny way of enduring when time and fate seem determined to keep it apart.

Family Ties

The love that parents, children, siblings, and close relatives have for each other often endures in profound ways. Family love can reunite and reconnect people, even after years apart or across generations. It reminds us to honor our origins and highlights that love is a thread woven through time, keeping us connected to our roots.

Love Across Lifetimes

Many cultures have their own age-old folk stories about love that transcend lifetimes. Reincarnation legends almost always include the idea of souls reuniting in subsequent incarnations despite all the odds. At the heart of reincarnation is the notion of souls meeting over and over in more than one lifetime. An inseverable link pulling one soul to another. Regardless of your belief in reincarnation, these are stunning reminders of the deep power of love.

## How Love Lives On After Loss

When someone we love has died, the pain of that loss can feel insurmountable, yet love is quite miraculous in its ability to endure. So, how do we continue to love when that person is no longer physically with us?

<u>Through the Memories</u>

Memories are one of the most meaningful ways love lives. The things we've done together, the laughter, the lessons learned—those all live within us and shape who we are. Each time we remember those we've lost, we hold their love in our hearts.

Through Legacy

Love also continues through the legacy people leave behind. Whether it's a tradition, a piece of wisdom, or even the kindness they've shown to others, the impact of love ripples outward. We carry their love forward in the way we live our lives and the way we treat others.

## Through Spiritual Connection

For many people, there is solace in knowing that love crosses over from the physical, and numerous tales of that love stretch long after a loved one passes. Whether it be a sign, a dream, or a feeling of presence, the connection inspires and infers that love is limitless.

## The Soul Contract Theory

One of the most intriguing concepts of love is the soul connection theory—the notion that love is a kind of force that exists on a soul level and transcends our physical existence. The soul connection theory or soul mate theory is found in many spiritual teachings and philosophies and offers an interesting perspective on the nature of love.

## Twin Flames and Soulmates

Many spiritual people believe in the idea of twin flames or "soulmates" whose souls are entwined on a spiritual level. Twin flames often refer to two halves of a soul that always meet and go through life together; soulmates are those whose souls are deeply connected and serve to help each other somehow.

Whether you believe in soul connections or not, the idea emphasizes how profound and meaningful our relationships can be.

## Love as energy

Some philosophies embrace the notion that love is a type of energy that exists eternally, neither created nor destroyed, but only transformed. It suggests that love continues in some way even after losing someone in a physical sense by, say, death, distance, or time.

## Universal love and oneness

The soul connection theory is also associated with the concept of universal love, a view that all souls are inherently intertwined. In this cosmology, love is not a specific relationship with another but rather an omnipresent force that connects all that exists.

## Why Love Beyond Death and Time Matters

The idea that love transcends death and time is more than just comforting—it's transformative. It reminds us that the connections we build in this life are eternal and that love is never truly lost. This perspective can strengthen us in times of grief, helping us honor the love we've shared and carry it forward.

Understanding love as a timeless force also inspires us to appreciate our time. When we realize that love is forever, we become more open, receptive, and willing to give and receive it in all its forms.

**Conclusion**: The Timelessness of Love is one of the only things in life that is truly timeless. Love is what ties us to the people we have lost, love is what connects us across generations, and love is what continues to reverberate outward long after we have gone. Love is boundless, whether by way of memories, legacy, or spiritual connection.

In the end, love reminds us of our shared humanity and of that enduring truth that no matter where we are or how we find ourselves at any moment, we are never truly alone. Love is, and always will be, the highest frequency of life, reverberating beyond time itself.

# Chapter 22:

# Practical Exercises on Love

Love is an extraordinary code of well-being and magic in and of itself. But just like with anything, it requires practice to intend love. To feel it deeply, cultivate it for yourself, your own being, another person in a relationship, or others and all humanity at large. Applying these practices patiently can make you start truly embodying love rather than just feel or think about it. Chapter 3 of the book presents a 30-Day Love Challenge to practice embodiment of love in daily life, tools from mirror work to affirmations to cultivating love for ourselves & others.

The 30-Day Love Challenge The 30-day love challenge is a transformative journey designed to help you focus on love every single day. Incorporating small but meaningful actions into your routine creates lasting habits that nurture love in all its forms. Here's a simple framework:

**Week 1: practicing Self-love and Self-compassion.**

Day 1: List 5 things that you love about yourself.

Day 2: Take 15 minutes to do something that brings you joy. Do it for yourself.

Day 3: Look at yourself in the mirror and say, "I love you!" to yourself.

Day 4: Set a boundary to protect your peace!

Day 5: Forgive yourself for a mistake you've been holding on to.

Day 6: Write down three unchanging things you're grateful for about yourself.

Day 7 :

**Week 2: Deepening Connections**

Day 8: Write a little thoughtful note to someone you love.

Day 9: Spend time with someone you love No mobiles or distractions, just you and them.

Day 10: Ask forgiveness from the person you hurt but still love.

Day 11: Tell someone in your family or a friend one thing that you like about them.

Day 12: Perform a small act of service for someone, such as making them a cup of tea or helping them with a task.

Day 13: Tell someone how much they mean to you in a genuine manner.

Day 14: Do something fun with somebody that you love.

**Week 3: Loving Strangers**

Day 15: Smile at everyone you pass today.

Day 16: Pay for a stranger's coffee or meal.

Day 17: Leave a kind note for someone to find.

Day 18: Volunteer your time.

Day 19: Compliment someone you don't know.

Day 20: Make a donation to a charity or cause that is important to you.

Day 21: Commit a random act of kindness, whether it's simply holding the door or letting someone go in front of you.

**Week 4 Universal Love and How to Live with It**

Day 22: Go outside and meditate on your connectedness to the rest of the world.

Day 23: Meditate for 10 minutes on the feeling of love and compassion.

Day 24: You can give back by ______

Day 25: Thank somebody who has made a difference in your life, even if it's been forever.

Day 26: Spend a conversation listening actively to the other person, giving them your full focused attention.

Day 27: Share something you're passionate about and inspire others with it.

Day 28: What does love mean to you? Write it

Day 29: Forgive someone you've been holding a grudge against.

Day 30: Celebrate the love journey you've been on and spread the joy. Mirror Work for Self-Love Mirror work promotes self-love by breaking down the barriers of self-doubt that act as blockades. Stare into your own eyes in the mirror, profess affirmations or words of love for yourself out loud. It might initially feel awkward or silly, but it can be transformational.

## How to Do Mirror Work

Find a place for yourself where you'll be undisturbed, and bring a mirror.

Look into your eyes and dig deep into yourself, say I love and accept myself exactly as I am out loud in these affirmations. "I love and accept myself exactly as I am." "I am worthy of love and happiness." "I am enough." Doing this for at least 5 minutes a day.

## Why this works

Mirror work rewires negative self-talk and lays down a new, positive foundation of reinforcement. Addressing yourself directly helps establish a deeper, more loving relationship with the exact person you are.

How Love Affirmations Can Work for You Affirmations are simple, positive statements that help focus your mind and influence your beliefs. When it comes to love, affirmations can be a powerful tool to attract and boost love in your life. Here's how you can make them work for you:

Make Custom Affirmations

Choose affirmations that resonate with you and your goals. Here are some examples:

"I radiate love, and others reflect love back to me." You are the image of love. "I am open to loving and receiving more of it daily." You are open to love. "I am worthy of love, trust, and kindness." You are worthy of love.

Integrate Them Into Your Routine

Write your affirmations in a journal every morning. Say your affirmations out loud when you do your mirror work.

Set alerts in your phone calendar to remind you to say your affirmations throughout the day.  5. Believe in them. Affirmations work best when you believe that what you're saying is true. It may feel strange or fake at first, but affirmations can shift the way you think and view yourself in love if you use them consistently and persist.

## Why Love Exercises Are Important

Love is both a noun and a verb. When you can practice love every day, it becomes a habit that fuels relationships, boosts well-being, and creates a ripple of goodness beyond your immediate circle. From an intentional practice to a structured challenge, here are some ways to practice love on a daily basis. Whether it's through an ongoing challenge, mirror work, or affirmations, these love exercises can help you live your life in a more loving, intentional, and joyful way.

Love is a journey, a lifelong journey. Like any journey, it takes work, patience, and practice. And that’s what these exercises are – practice. Through these exercises, we practice living in love. None of these things is about being perfect, and sometimes it’s difficult to see someone broad smiling beside something all the time, particularly if we’re going through our own struggles. This is not about that at all. But as long as we practise and try, we are going to get there to a life full of love.

As you move forward, remember that love is a gift and a choice. It's something you cultivate, give, receive, and expand. And the more you do, the more love you will find in your relationships, yourself, and the world around you.

Sorry, forgiveness, gratitude, and love. These are the four pillars of happiness, without which we can't truly be happy. Sorry, forgiveness, gratitude, and love heal our wounds, connect us to the beauty of life, and provide meaning tomorrow. Let us now discuss how we can incorporate them into our lives, the lasting effect of living by these four pillars, and the bottom-line takeaway: happiness is a choice.

# SUMMARY

**In conclusion,** let us recap what we have discussed in this soul journey and healing essay. The four pillars of inner peace are sorry (remorse and self-accountability), forgiveness, gratitude, and love. These are the foundational components of creating a peaceful and purposeful life. Where we find peace within ourselves, we can extend that peace to others and the world around us.

**Sorry (Remorse and Self-Accountability)**

True Teshuva arises from sincere remorse for our actions and a genuine acceptance of responsibility. Saying sorry goes beyond mere apology; it demonstrates our intent to improve by acknowledging our faults. When we are truly sorry and amend our wrongs, we liberate ourselves from guilt and strengthen our connections with those around us. When we genuinely take responsibility for our actions, we live as free individuals with a sense of integrity and accountability.

**Forgiveness**

Holding onto resentment is a burden carried in your heart. The only way to find inner peace is by forgiving those who have hurt you in the past. It's not about saying that what they did to you was okay or that you'll forget what they've done. However, releasing yourself from the negativity you feel towards them will truly set you free. Forgiving those who trespass against you—and, most importantly, forgiving yourself—can help you heal and create space for a new chapter.

**Gratitude.**

Contentment comes when we shift our focus from what we want to what we have. Shift your focus with gratitude—a thankful heart is a happy heart. Gratitude helps us see the beauty of the present moment and be joyful for life's simple treasures. With daily gratitude, we foster a mindset of abundance and positive thinking, which allows peace to flow freely in our lives.

**Love**

Love is the highest vibration. It's the ultimate state of inner peace. When we move through life leading with love (for ourselves, for others, and for the world as a whole), fear falls away. Separation falls away. Love shows us how to be kind. How to be patient. How to accept everything as it is. It opens us up to deeper, more meaningful ways of relating to each other. It reminds us of our oneness. In a state of unconditional love, the soul gets what it has always craved. True fulfillment. And our foundation of peace is unshakable.

Here , .

The Hawaiian lifestyle is a life built on four pillars: Remorse, where there is an apology; forgiveness; gratitude, and love that help you live a peaceful and meaningful life. They help the individual to "let go" of the load that is no longer there, to welcome his present life with gratitude, to give and receive love, and to be wholly and completely responsible in his or her life.

# ABOUT AUTHOR

Dr. Muneer Jan is a passionate advocate for inner peace, healing, and personal growth. With a background in medicine(anesthesiology and critical care specialist) and a deep understanding of human emotions, he blends wisdom, compassion, and practical insights to help readers navigate life's challenges.

Through his writing, Dr. Muneer Jan inspires individuals to embrace forgiveness, gratitude, love, and the power of saying sorry as pathways to true peace. His work reflects a lifelong dedication to both the science of healing and the art of inner transformation.

When he's not writing, Dr. Muneer Jan enjoys sharing knowledge, guiding others on their journey to self-discovery, and making a meaningful impact in the lives of those around him.

# Acknowledgment

First, I want to thank my mother for her wisdom, love, teachings, inspiration, determination, strength, tenacity, moral fiber, and her boundless support heart. She embodies the soulfulness and choice, the reality and renewal, that have forged a pathway grounded in the belief that one can achieve anything if one sets their mind to it and works hard. You are the foundation for whatever song lives within me.

I would also like to take this opportunity to thank my family and friends for their continued support and encouragement throughout this period. Their faith in me and their patience during my long hours of writing have enabled me to achieve this goal.

To the mentors and teachers I have had along the way who, through what they shared of their insights and perspectives, enriched my understanding of life that shaped the ideas of this book.

Finally, thank you, the reader, for allowing me to share this journey. I hope the lessons in these pages resonate with you and help you find your path to inner peace.

With gratitude,

Dr.Muneer Jan

# Disclaimer

The four pillars of inner peace, Saying Sorry, Forgiveness, Gratitude, and Love, offered in this book are guidelines to help you develop these four principles. These guidelines are for inspiration and informational purposes only.

This book does not substitute for competent psychological, medical, or legal advice. Each person's journey to inner peace is different, and no one can predict the extent to which these principles will be effective for you. If you are suffering from emotional distress, trauma, or mental health problems, you deserve to have the support of a competent therapist, counselor, or health care provider.

The author and publisher of this book disclaim any responsibility or liability whatsoever for the interpretation or use of the ideas, concepts, or information discussed. While applying the pillars is bound to empower a more peacefully fulfilling life, ultimately, the onus is on the reader to carefully think and apply them where relevant and seek professional and personal guidance where necessary.

By reading this book, you acknowledge that you are solely responsible for using this content..

# References and Scientific Studies

Lazare, A. (2005). On Apology. Oxford University Press.

1. Schumann, K. (2014). "The Psychology of Offering an Apology: Understanding Why We Apologize." Current Directions in Psychological Science.
2. Goffman, E. (1971). Relations in Public: Microstudies of the Public Order. Harper.
3. Tavuchis, N. (1991). Mea Culpa: A Sociology of Apology and Reconciliation. Stanford University Press.

4. Exline, J. J., et al. (2011). "Forgiveness, Apology, and Repair: Have You Reconciled After a Conflict?" Journal of Personality and Social Psychology.

5. Brown, B. (2012). Daring Greatly: How the Courage to Be Vulnerable Transforms the Way We Live. Penguin.

6. Okimoto, T. G., & Wenzel, M. (2014). "Apologies and Forgiveness: Understanding the Challenges of Interpersonal Healing." Social Psychological and Personality Science.

7. Byrne, R. W., et al. (2001). "The Role of Empathy in Apology Acceptance." Behavioral Sciences.

8. Cohen, T. R., et al. (2014). "Apology, Trust, and Forgiveness: A Closer Examination of the Interplay." Negotiation and Conflict Management Research.

9. Freedman, S. R., & Enright, R. D. (1996). "Forgiveness as an Intervention Goal with Incest Survivors." Journal of Consulting and Clinical Psychology.

10. Haidt, J. (2006). The Happiness Hypothesis: Finding Modern Truth in Ancient Wisdom. Basic Books.

11. Frantz, C. M., & Bennet, A. (2006). "The Role of Apology in Restorative Justice." Behavioral Sciences and Law.

12. Komorita, S. S. (1980). "Cooperative Interaction in Apology Settings." Journal of Conflict Resolution.

13. Scher, S. J., & Darley, J. M. (1997). "How Effective Are the Things People Say to Apologize?" Journal of Social Psychology.

14. Wohl, M. J. A., & Branscombe, N. R. (2005). "Forgiveness and Apology in Intergroup Conflict Resolution." Personality and Social Psychology Bulletin.

15. Pettigrove, G. (2009). "Apology, Forgiveness, and Moral Repair." Ethics.

16. Gold, G. J., & Weiner, B. (2000). "Apology Effects on

Responsibility Attributions and Forgiveness." Journal of Personality and Social Psychology.

17. Levine, R. V., et al. (2001). "Cultural Differences in Apology Expressions." Journal of Language and Social Psychology.

18. Kim, P. H., et al. (2004). "The Effects of Apology and Power on Forgiveness." Journal of Management.

19. Risen, J. L., & Gilovich, T. (2007). "Target and Observer Perspectives on Apologies." Journal of Personality and Social Psychology.

20. Forgiveness: The Path to Freedom

21. Worthington, E. L., Jr. (2003). Forgiving and Reconciling: Bridges to Wholeness and Hope. InterVarsity Press.

22. McCullough, M. E., et al. (1997). "Interpersonal Forgiving in Close Relationships." Journal of Personality and Social Psychology.

23. Luskin, F. (2003). Forgive for Good: A Proven Prescription for Health and Happiness. HarperOne.

24. Enright, R. D. (2001). Forgiveness Is a Choice: A Step-by-Step Process for Resolving Anger and Restoring Hope. APA LifeTools.

25. Toussaint, L. L., et al. (2001). "Forgiveness and Health: An

Exploration of Pathways." Journal of Behavioral Medicine.

26. Smedes, L. B. (1996). The Art of Forgiving: When You Need to Forgive and Don't Know How. Ballantine Books.

27. Rye, M. S., et al. (2001). "The Efficacy of Forgiveness Interventions in Women Recovering from Spousal Emotional Abuse." Journal of Consulting and Clinical Psychology.

28. Davis, D. E., et al. (2015). "Trait Forgiveness and Interpersonal Adjustment." Personality and Individual Differences.

29. Karremans, J. C., et al. (2003). "Forgiveness and Relationship

Longevity." Journal of Social and Personal Relationships.

30. Lawler, K. A., et al. (2003). "A Change of Heart: Cardiovascular Correlates of Forgiveness in Response to Interpersonal Conflict." Journal of Behavioral Medicine.

31. Baumeister, R. F., et al. (1998). "Interpersonal Aspects of Forgiveness and Revenge." Advances in Social Cognition.

32. Exline, J. J., & Baumeister, R. F. (2000). "Forgiveness as Emotion-Focused Coping." Journal of Personality and Social Psychology.

33. Hargrave, T. D. (1994). Families and Forgiveness: Healing

Wounds in the Intergenerational Family. Routledge.

34. Wade, N. G., & Worthington, E. L., Jr. (2003). "Forgiveness in Therapy." Journal of Clinical Psychology.

35. Paleari, F. G., et al. (2005). "Forgiveness and Satisfaction in Close Relationships." Journal of Personality and Social Psychology.

36. Fincham, F. D., & Beach, S. R. H. (2002). "Forgiveness in Marriage." Journal of Family Psychology.

37. Hall, J. H., & Fincham, F. D. (2005). "Self-Forgiveness: The Stepchild of Forgiveness Research."

Journal of Social and Clinical Psychology.

38. Coyle, C. T., & Enright, R. D. (1997). "Forgiveness Intervention with Postabortion Men." Journal of Consulting and Clinical Psychology.

39. Sandage, S. J., & Worthington, E. L., Jr. (2010). "Forgiveness, Relationships, and Well-Being." Journal of Counseling Psychology.

40. Kornfield, J. (1993). A Path with Heart: A Guide Through the Perils and Promises of Spiritual Life. Bantam.

41. Gratitude: The Foundation of Joy

9 789334 236163

Printed at Repro India Ltd.